WORTH
WAITING FOR

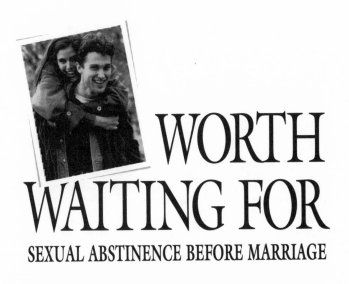

WORTH WAITING FOR

SEXUAL ABSTINENCE BEFORE MARRIAGE

BRENT A. BARLOW

DESERET BOOK COMPANY
SALT LAKE CITY, UTAH

Dedication

This book is dedicated to the "pure people" the Lord will raise up to serve him in righteousness in the last days. (D&C 100:16.)

Quotations on page 26 from *Mandate for Change,* ed. Will Marshall and Martin Schram. Copyright © 1993 by Progressive Policy Institute. Used by permission of the Putnam Publishing Group.

Quotations on pages 27–28 from *Learn to Discern* by Robert G. DeMoss, Jr. Copyright © 1992 by Robert G. DeMoss, Jr. Used by permission of Zondervan Publishing House.

Library of Congress Cataloging-in-Publication Data

Barlow, Brent A., 1941–
    Worth waiting for : sexual abstinence before marriage / Brent A. Barlow.
        p.   cm.
    Includes bibliographical references and index.
    ISBN 0-87579-920-5
    1. Sexual abstinence—Religious aspects—Church of Jesus Christ of
Latter-day Saints. 2. Sex—Religious aspects—Church of Jesus
Christ of Latter-day Saints. 3. Single people—Sexual behavior.
4. Sexual ethics. I. Title.
HQ63.B37   1995
241'.66—dc20   94-40476
                                                                                    CIP

Printed in the United States of America
10 9   8   7   6   5   4   3   2   1

See that ye bridle all your passions,
that ye may be filled with love.

ALMA 38:12

Let virtue garnish thy thoughts unceasingly;
then shall thy confidence wax strong in the
presence of God. . . . The Holy Ghost shall be
thy constant companion, and thy scepter an
unchanging scepter of righteousness and truth;
and thy dominion shall be an everlasting
dominion, and without compulsory means it
shall flow unto thee forever and ever.

D&C 121:45–46; EMPHASIS ADDED

Contents

Contents

Acknowledgments

As with other books I have written, I am indebted to many people who have helped me organize my thoughts and ideas to create *Worth Waiting For: Sexual Abstinence before Marriage.*

First and foremost, I would like to thank my many students at Brigham Young University. Over the years they have shared with me, both in the classroom and privately, their interests, hopes, and concerns regarding sexual behavior. Their comments and observations have given me my main interest in writing this book.

I would like to thank Jay A. Parry, editor of this book, who has dealt with some rather sensitive material while editing this book. The more I write, the more I appreciate the perceptivity and skills of editors such as Jay Parry. In addition, Emily Watts and other editors reviewed the initial draft of this book and gave helpful recommendations for its continued refinement. I also appreciate and give thanks to other individuals at Deseret Book who have worked on this book in some way; these include Sheri Dew, Michelle Eckersley, Devan Jensen, Ronald Millett, and Patricia J. Parkinson.

My thanks to Chanalin S. Prina, a teaching assistant and English major at BYU, who has now assisted in editing the last three books I have written. I appreciate her insightful contributions as she has helped me prepare the manuscript for publication. Thanks also to my other current teaching assistants, Sydney Smith, David Dastrup, and Warren Price, for timely suggestions and comments.

Dr. Terrance D. Olson, chairman of the Department of Family Sciences at Brigham Young University and a personal friend, has again given support and encouragement. Thanks also to JanaLee Romrell and Bea Jasperson, department staff members, for their encouragement as well.

I thank my five children remaining at home, Brian, Jon, Jason, Kristin, and Brandon, who have all been both patient and supportive while the book was being written.

And finally, I thank my wife, Susan, for her practical approach to life and her concern for the well-being, growth, and development of young people. Her common sense, sensitivity, and counsel regarding the creation of a book of this nature have been deeply appreciated.

Introduction

SEXUAL ABSTINENCE: ARE WE DEPARTING FROM THE FAITH?

For some time I have felt that I would like to write a book on the great blessing of sexual abstinence before marriage. Over a seventeen-year period I've shared my feelings and observations on this subject with some ten thousand of my students at Brigham Young University.

But it was a late-night phone call not long ago that gave me my final impetus. It was from one of my students in the "Preparation for Marriage" class I teach at BYU. She asked if we could talk for a few minutes and indicated she wanted to remain anonymous. I soon understood why she made that request.

The young woman paused for a moment and then informed me that she and her fiancé had become sexually involved with each other, even though they planned to be married in the Provo Temple in only two months. Now she was worried that they might not be worthy to go to the temple. I told her I understood her concern. But then she said her fiancé had instructed her that she must not tell their bishop what they had done. In fact, he told her that she must lie in their forthcoming temple recommend interview.

That concerned me greatly. I've been around many single Latter-day Saints for the past two decades, and I'm well aware that some young couples step past the boundaries of propriety in their premarital relationships. But I was particularly disturbed that their transgression didn't seem to trouble her future husband.

My anonymous student on the phone continued: "My fiancé asked me a straightforward, simple question: 'Why wait?' We'll be married in only a few weeks. What difference does it make if we start to be intimate now? And he argued that many other young couples are doing the same thing." She hesitated and then continued. "He also said it was not necessary to confess to the bishop or the stake president. We'll work it out ourselves with the Lord after we're married."

Since I was serving as an LDS bishop at the time of the phone call, I told the student that the temple recommend interview asked plainly if the applicant was honest. How, I asked, could both she and her fiancé lie to their bishop during the interview process? I suggested she go back to her fiancé and encourage him to reconsider his suggestion. There was a great moral inconsistency, I suggested, in lying to get a recommend to go to the temple.

Before she hung up, I suggested there were many good reasons for waiting until marriage for sexual relationships. I also said that if her fiancé insisted on lying to the bishop to get a temple recommend, she may want to reconsider his proposal of marriage.

My student thanked me for taking time to talk to her and hung up. I went right to bed, but I didn't go to sleep for a long time. I kept replaying the conversation in my mind—along with similar conversations I'd recently had with a few other young

Latter-day Saints. They all asked me the same question: "Why wait?" Some felt that (1) sexual behavior prior to marriage no longer mattered, or mattered less than in "less enlightened times"; (2) it was no longer necessary to "confess" one's sins to either a bishop or stake president; (3) that sexual impropriety before marriage was now quite common and "many others are doing it"; and (4) (and perhaps most disturbing) that "we'll work it out ourselves. It is just a matter between us and the Lord."

As I tossed and turned in my attempt to sleep that night I began to wonder if such questions, attitudes, and behaviors were becoming more common in the Church. Is there now less sexual restraint before marriage? Are some Latter-day Saints, both old and young, now asking the question "Why wait?" Are they being affected by trends outside the Church? Do young Latter-day Saints now believe that "everyone is doing it"—and use that as partial justification and rationalization for their errant behavior? I wondered about three o'clock that morning how common it was to believe that it is no longer necessary to confess one's sins to a priesthood leader. I later reread Doctrine and Covenants 58:43, which says that true repentance involves both confessing and forsaking the sin. In addition, Doctrine and Covenants 64:7 teaches that the Lord forgives serious sins only after they are confessed, and Doctrine and Covenants 59:12 makes clear that we must confess to the appropriate Church leaders as well as to the Lord. I also recalled that President Spencer W. Kimball saw confession as so crucial a part of the repentance process that he devoted one whole chapter to the topic in his book *The Miracle of Forgiveness.* (See Chapter 13, "Lifting Burdens Through Confession" [Salt Lake City: Bookcraft, 1969], pp. 177–90.) Why have some young Latter-day Saints been led to believe that their behavior is really "only between them and the Lord"?

It Doesn't Matter Anymore

A few days after the phone call another student came into my office at BYU and said he wanted to talk to me. He told me he had recently returned from a mission and was dating a young woman in his singles ward at BYU. He said she was attractive, active in the Church, and held a responsible ward calling. They had dated several weeks and had maintained a proper relationship, but over the weekend that had begun to change. Toward the end of their date, they were sharing appropriate types of affection when she became sexually aggressive and started doing things he thought were inappropriate. He said he told her that what she was doing was not right and her simple reply was, "It doesn't matter anymore. Everyone does it." She truly had her conscience "seared with a hot iron," as the scriptures indicated would happen in the last days. (1 Tim. 4:1–3.) They ended the date, but he was puzzled and concerned, not only over her inappropriate sexual actions but also by her rationalization that she was doing nothing wrong.

He asked me what I thought. I observed that I had always been saddened to see how some young men were aggressive in seeking inappropriate sexual activity—and now we were seeing some young women do the same thing. I told him that he should unquestionably tell her that *it does still matter,* perhaps more today than ever before! (See Morm. 8:31.) His generation, I suggested, did not invent either sex or sin, but like others before and since, they still will have to be accountable before the Lord for their actions. Since inappropriate sexual behavior before marriage can be initiated by either male or female, I suggested he go home and review Genesis 39 about Joseph and Potiphar's wife. If the young woman he was dating continued her advances "day by day" (v. 10), he ought to do as Joseph of old did—leave her and the circumstances she was creating.

Of course, I don't believe that the attitudes expressed in that late-night phone call or that office visit represent the attitudes held by most of the students at BYU. On the contrary, I have been impressed with the efforts most BYU students are making to live gospel principles, in spite of real temptations. Yet at the same time I have become aware that the world's liberal attitudes toward sexual behavior are beginning to influence some young people in the Church.

Attaining Happiness

Think for a moment. What is it you want out of life? Is it wealth? Security? Peace of mind? A good marriage? Close relationships with your children? A good job? Fame? Power? Free time? Spiritual development? Friends? More ability to help others? Personal possessions? Travel to exciting places?

Where does happiness fit in your list? How important is happiness to you? Look around you. How many people are happy? How many are miserable? Is Satan accomplishing his plan of making all "miserable like unto himself"? (2 Ne. 2:27.)

If we as human beings have any universal goals, at the top of the list would be happiness, contentment, and peace of mind. The Prophet Joseph Smith once noted:

"Happiness is the object and design of our existence; and will be the end thereof, if we pursue the path that leads to it; and this path is *virtue, uprightness, faithfulness, holiness, and keeping all the commandments of God.*" (*Teachings of the Prophet Joseph Smith*, selected by Joseph Fielding Smith [Salt Lake City: Deseret Book Co., 1938], pp. 255–56; italics added.)

Similarly, King Benjamin observed in the Book of Mormon:

"Consider on the blessed and happy state of those that keep the commandments of God. For behold, they are blessed in all things, both temporal and spiritual; and if they hold out faithful to the end they are received into heaven, that thereby they may dwell with God in a state of never-ending happiness.

O remember, remember that these things are true; for the Lord God hath spoken it." (Mosiah 2:41.)

Perhaps we, too, may become like the Nephites of old and "owe all our happiness" to the "sacred word of God." (Alma 44:5.)

Need of the Spirit in Our Lives

Besides attaining personal happiness and avoiding all the unpleasant, painful consequences of sexual indiscretion, there are some additional important reasons Latter-day Saints need to practice sexual restraint before marriage in these last days.

In 1914 President Joseph F. Smith warned of some trends that could greatly harm the Church. He stated:

> There are at least three dangers that threaten the Church *within,* and the authorities need to awaken to the fact that the people should be warned unceasingly against them. As I see these, they are (1) flattery of prominent men in the world; (2) false educational ideas; and (3) sexual impurity. But the third subject mentioned—personal purity, is perhaps of greater importance than either of the other two. . . . If purity of life is neglected, all other dangers set in upon us like the rivers of waters when the flood gates are opened. (*Improvement Era,* 17 [March 1914]:476. Quoted in *Gospel Doctrine: Sermons and Writings of President Joseph F. Smith* [Salt Lake City: Deseret News Press, 1919], pp. 391–92; italics added.)

Now compare President Joseph F. Smith's warning with the concern voiced by President Ezra Taft Benson: "No sin is causing the loss of the Spirit of the Lord among our people more today than sexual promiscuity. It is causing our people to stumble, damning their growth, darkening their spiritual powers, and making them subject to other sins." (*The Teachings of Ezra Taft Benson* [Salt Lake City: Bookcraft, 1988], p. 279.)

On another occasion he said: "A reason for virtue—which includes personal chastity, clean thoughts and practices, and integrity—*is that we must have the Spirit and the power of God in our lives to do God's work.* Without that power and influence we are no better off than individuals in other organizations. That virtue shines through and will influence others toward a better life and cause nonmembers to inquire of our faith." (Ibid., pp. 278–79; italics added.)

LDS Church Leaders Reaffirm Sexual Standards

The importance of sexual abstinence before marriage and fidelity afterwards was reemphasized in 1990 by the First Presidency of the Church. They declared:

> Our Heavenly Father has counseled that sexual intimacy should be reserved for his children within the bonds of marriage. The physical relationship between a husband and a wife can be beautiful and sacred. It is ordained of God for the procreation of children and for the expression of love within a marriage: "Therefore shall a man leave his father and his mother, and shall cleave unto his wife; and they shall be one flesh." (Genesis 2:24.)
>
> Because sexual intimacy is so sacred, the Lord requires self-control and purity before marriage as well as full fidelity after marriage. In dating, treat your date with respect, and expect your date to show that same respect to you. Never treat your date as an object to be used for your own lustful desires or ego. Improper physical contact can cause a loss of self-control. Always stay in control of yourself and your physical feelings.
>
> The Lord specifically forbids certain behaviors,

including all sexual relations before marriage, petting, sex perversions (such as homosexuality, rape, and incest), masturbation, or preoccupation with sex in thought, speech, or action. . . .

You are responsible to make right choices. Whether directed toward those of the same or opposite gender, lustful feelings and desires may lead to more serious sins. All Latter-day Saints must learn to control and discipline themselves.

Victims of rape, incest, or other sexual abuses are not guilty of sin. If you have been a victim of any of these terrible crimes, be assured that God still loves you! Your bishop can also help and guide you through the mental and emotional healing process if you seek his advice and counsel.

Scripture reinforces the foregoing teachings and standards: "This I say then, Walk in the Spirit, and ye shall not fulfil the lust of the flesh. For the flesh lusteth against the Spirit, and the Spirit against the flesh: and these are contrary the one to the other: so that ye cannot do the things that ye would. . . . Now the works of the flesh are manifest, which are these; adultery, fornication, uncleanness, lasciviousness, . . . and such like: of the which I tell you before, as I have also told you in time past, that they which do such things shall not inherit the kingdom of God." (Galatians 5:16–17, 19–21.) (*For the Strength of Youth* [Salt Lake City: The Church of Jesus Christ of Latter-day Saints, 1990], pp. 14–16. Used by permission.)

Let's Do Something!

I have always been impressed with the admonitions that Latter-day Saints should be "doers of the word, and not hearers only."

(James 1:22.) James also counseled, "Therefore to him that knoweth to do good, and doeth it not, to him it is sin." (James 4:17.) The Savior promised at the conclusion of the Sermon on the Mount that "whosoever heareth these sayings of mine, *and doeth them*" would survive turbulent times in the last days. He also warned of the consequences of those that hear but "doeth them not." (See Matt. 7:24–28; italics added.)

Latter-day Saints, young and old, should therefore be people of action. I have often felt that "LDS" could also mean "Let's Do Something!" It is my hope that those who read this book will not just be "readers only" but will be "doers" as well, applying the gospel principles of chastity as they've been given in the scriptures and by Church leaders.

When given a particularly difficult task to perform, Nephi responded with five words: "I will go and do." Why was he so positive? Because he knew "the Lord giveth no commandments unto the children of men, save he shall prepare a way for them that they may accomplish the thing which he commandeth them." (1 Ne. 3:7.) This can also be our attitude with all that the Lord has commanded.

For Whom Is This Book Intended?

This book was written with several audiences in mind:

1. **PARENTS.** LDS parents have a mandate from latter-day revelation to teach their children gospel principles. (See D&C 68:25–28.) As we'll discuss in detail in Chapter 6, recent research indicates that parents are still critical teachers and sources of information of a sexual nature for their children.

2. **GRANDPARENTS.** Scripture indicates that in ancient Israel, adults were to teach not only their own children but also their "sons' sons" and, by implication, their "daughters' daughters." (See Deut. 4:9; 6:2.) Perhaps the same is still true in modern Israel. Latter-day Saint grandparents may play an increasingly

important role in teaching young people values during the chaotic years ahead.

3. TEACHERS AND YOUTH LEADERS. Latter-day Saints have been commanded to "teach one another" gospel truths. (See D&C 88:118.) Some, like myself, may teach as a career or profession. Others may teach young people as a Church calling or ecclesiastical stewardship. In addition, the scriptures and statements of Latter-day prophets used in this book may help as we seek, as missionaries, to teach the law of chastity to those who are not yet members of the Church.

4. ENGAGED COUPLES. Most engaged couples have a particularly difficult time controlling their sexual impulses, even though they may have been able to do so prior to the engagement. This is often true for young LDS engaged couples as well. Following some of the suggestions provided in Chapter 7, "Difficulties during Engagement," may be helpful.

5. TEENAGERS AND YOUNG ADULTS. Alma admonished, "Learn wisdom in thy youth; yea, learn in thy youth to keep the commandments of God." (Alma 37:35.) The teen and young adult years are a crucial time of life when many decisions regarding sexual behavior are being made. In addition, young people can often help their friends as they deal with these questions. Teenagers and young adults, therefore, may benefit by reading this book not only for their own information but also to help them assist others with these decisions as the need arises. The Apostle Paul wrote that if anyone "be overtaken in a fault, ye which are spiritual, restore such an one in the spirit of meekness; considering thyself, lest thou also be tempted." (Gal. 6:1.)

Chapter 1

THE LAST DAYS AND THE SECOND SEXUAL REVOLUTION

Most people are aware that during the late 1960s and the 1970s America underwent what has been called the "Sexual Revolution." As the post-World War II Baby Boomers entered the teen years and became young adults, sexual restraint was often set aside. Young people seemed less inclined to wait until marriage for sexual relations. Consequently, once married, fewer saw the necessity of confining sexual activity only to a husband or wife, and extramarital sexual experiences dramatically increased in the years that followed. Homosexual and other sexual activities also became more prominent or open during this same period.

What many may not be aware of, however, is that during the past decade, 1983 to 1993, we have undergone a Second Sexual Revolution in this country. The advent of AIDS (Acquired Immune Deficiency Syndrome) in the early 1980s may, ironically, have been a major contributing factor to the increase of sexual activity, particularly among the teenagers in this country. In our concern to educate young people about the perils of AIDS and other sexually transmitted diseases, we may have overwhelmed them with a steady flow of sex information without also presenting adequate guidelines or values regarding sexual behavior.

Let's look back a few years to see how we got to where we are now.

A Critical Year

Where were you in 1968? Many of you weren't even born yet. Some were just young children or teenagers. Others were at various stages of life. My wife, Susan, and I had been married three years and had one child, Doug. In July 1968, we strapped him into the backseat of our 1965 Chevy, loaded our luggage, said goodbye to our parents, and drove from Utah to Tallahassee, Florida, where I began my doctoral studies in marriage and family living.

The transition to Florida State University and graduate school was a difficult adjustment for me in more ways than one. I grew up in the small Mormon community of Centerfield, Utah, and had lived in Utah all my life, except for the years of my LDS mission to Scotland and Ireland. I had attended and graduated from BYU and later taught seminary in Kaysville, Utah.

Up until 1968, my whole life—including my studies and my work—had been involved with Latter-day Saints. Now I had some apprehension about moving out "into the world" and studying in a non-LDS setting. What would we find in our movement from Zion to the world? Would we witness all the worldly trends we'd heard about? Or would we find others much like ourselves, with similar concerns and values regarding marriage and family?

Actually, we found both. During my first year at Florida State, I witnessed frequent student protests over the war in Vietnam. Lack of sexual restraint was flaunted both on and off campus. Students were arrested for "streaking" or running naked through the campus. Others were apprehended by campus police for bathing nude in the large fountain pools on campus.

After graduating in 1971, I accepted a position to teach at Southern Illinois University at Carbondale, Illinois. While teaching at both Florida State and Southern Illinois University, I had some interesting experiences in the classroom. Many of my students openly advocated premarital and extramarital sex, along with other "alternative lifestyles." Coarse words referring to sexual activity were sometimes used in class. Student dress standards were "relaxed," to say the least, and were sometimes provocative.

Many other students, graduate students, and faculty, however, were much like myself. They had been brought up with conventional and conservative family values, often as a result of their religious training. They believed in chastity and modesty just as I did. (I'd like to note here that the word *chastity* is not commonly used by many young people and, when used, means different things to different people. For instance, my dictionary indicates that chastity may mean "purity in conduct," "restraint and simplicity," or "personal integrity." I use the term in its primary meaning: "abstention from unlawful sexual intercourse.")

The Second Sexual Revolution

In some ways, then, I observed firsthand the beginnings of the First Sexual Revolution. The Second Sexual Revolution has been more subtle and is just now becoming evident.

In 1993, two doctors, Samuel S. Janus, Ph.D., and his wife, Cynthia L. Janus, M.D., published *The Janus Report on Sexual Behavior* (New York: John Wiley and Sons, 1993). Some claim it is the most comprehensive study of sexual behavior since the Kinsey reports on human sexuality of the male (1948) and the female (1953).

In the preface to their book they note that "a Second Sexual

Revolution has now taken place," which includes "a willingness to engage in a variety of sexual practices, some of which may once have been deemed deviant or at least unacceptable to one's social status." (P. vii.)

This revolution seems to have affected almost all age groups and social segments of our society. But it particularly seems to have influenced our youth. Survey after survey shows the same thing: The youth of America are more sexually active than ever before, and they're starting at a younger age.

According to a cover article in *Time* magazine, "By the time they are 20, three-quarters of young Americans have had sex." ("Kids, Sex and Values," *Time,* May 24, 1993, p. 61.)

Unfortunately, religious activity only slightly curtails sexual relationships before marriage. In one 1993 study, only(!) 71 percent of the "very religious" reported sexual relationships before marriage, compared to 93 percent who were "not religious." (*The Janus Report*, p. 252.)

A 1988 National Survey of Family Growth found that 25 percent of females had had sexual relationships by age 15 and 80 percent by age 19. A 1988 National Survey of Young Men found that by age 15, 33 percent of males had had sexual relationships and by age 19 the number had risen to 86 percent. Thus, according to these two studies, 80 percent of females and 86 percent of males have had sexual intercourse by age 19. (Frank D. Cox, *Human Intimacy: Marriage, The Family and Its Meaning* [New York: West Publishing Company, 1993], p. 105.)

The Janus Report also observed:

Meanwhile, youngsters were experimenting with their own sexuality at earlier and earlier ages. Barely out of their own childhood, teenagers were producing babies at ever-growing rates. By the 1980s, nearly a million mothers under 18 were giving birth every year. Of these young women, 70 percent were unmarried, up from 30 percent only a decade earlier. Some estimates indicate that as many as 10,000 extremely young women, age 12 or even younger, become pregnant every year. (P. 16.)

Janus and Janus concluded: "Sexual experience comes much earlier today, for more people, than in any previous era of our history." (P. 37.)

Religious Conformity and Sexual Behavior

One of the interesting aspects of *The Janus Report* was its study on the role of religion and how it affected the sexual behavior of the respondents. "Our observation," reported the two doctors, "is that Americans fit religion into their lives, rather than fitting their lives into the framework created by religion." (P. 389.)

Those who were questioned were divided into two periods of response: 1983–85 and 1988–92. They were then asked: "How important is it that your sexual practices are in harmony with your religious teachings?" Among those who reported between 1983 and 1985, 50 percent of both the men and the women indicated it was "very important" or "important." When the same question was asked of the group reporting between 1988 and 1992, the percentage fell to only 35 percent of the men and 38 percent of the women. Of this trend, the authors reported:

"Organized religions have traditionally had a dominant stake in the sexual lives of their adherents. . . . *Our respondents, while increasing a commitment to the importance of religion in marriage, increasingly rejected religious control over personal sexual expression.*" (P. 389; italics added.)

This trend, if true, gives new insights to the anonymous phone call and the office visit I described in the introduction. It also presents additional challenges to religious denominations such as The Church of Jesus Christ of Latter-day Saints and others who still strive to teach sexual abstinence before marriage.

Immorality in the Last Days

It should come as no surprise to us that sexual immorality would reach epidemic proportions in the last days—the Lord's prophets clearly saw that as one of the conditions of the last days. Moroni noted that the Book of Mormon would come forth when there were "great pollutions upon the face of the earth," along with murders, robbing, lying, deceivings, whoredoms, and "all manner of abominations." And those who commit such acts would declare "Do this, or do that, *and it mattereth not,* for the Lord will uphold such at the last day." (See Morm. 8:31; italics added.)

In speaking of the pollutions that have been prophesied, President Spencer W. Kimball observed:

> We talk of pollution with oil slicks, of cans and bottles, of waste paper everywhere, of indestructible plastic, old car bodies, or pesticides and smoke, and industrial wastes; but pollution is not only in the realm of physical. The more serious pollution is in the spiritual and mental phases of our lives. There is lewdness and licentiousness; there is pornography and V.D.; there is pollution growing everywhere in men's minds and their souls are contaminated.
>
> Thou shalt not commit adultery. Thou shalt not commit fornication. Thou shalt not commit sexual perversions. Thou shalt not be guilty of petting nor do anything like unto it. When a generation lives for sex and translates every message into that language, what can be expected of its people?
>
> The importance and necessity of virtue, real virtue,

total virtue, is as old as the inhabited world. If we had the record we would probably find that Cain was promiscuous, for seldom do great crimes travel in single file. (*Teachings of Spencer W. Kimball,* ed. Edward L. Kimball [Salt Lake City: Bookcraft, 1982], p. 268.)

Paul Writes about the Last Days

The Apostle Paul had some of the same understandings about the conditions that would exist before Christ's second coming. To Timothy he wrote:

"In the last days perilous times shall come. For men shall be lovers of their own selves, . . . *without natural affection,* . . . *incontinent,* . . . despisers of those that are good, . . . *lovers of pleasures more than lovers of God;* Having a form of godliness, but denying the power thereof; *from such turn away.*" (2 Tim. 3:1–5; italics added.)

The word *incontinent* means "unrestrained or uncontrolled in seeking sexual gratification." The Revised Standard Version of the Bible uses the word *profligate,* which means "utterly and shamelessly immoral and indifferent to moral restraints." Paul also saw that in our day people would be lovers or seekers of intense pleasure, perhaps in the forms of entertainment and recreation. Regarding all these, Paul wisely counsels, "from such turn away."

Some to Depart from the Faith

The Apostle Paul also wrote: "Now the Spirit speaketh expressly, that in the latter times *some shall depart from the faith,* giving heed to seducing spirits, and doctrines of devils; Speaking lies in hypocrisy, *having their conscience seared with a hot iron; Forbidding [or seeing no need?] to marry. . . .*" (1 Tim. 4:1–3; italics added.)

Of this latter passage, President Kimball, again, has noted:

Society has accepted immorality as normal. In the latter times some shall depart from the faith, said Paul. (See 1 Timothy 4:1.) These are the latter times. We are the Latter-day Saints. These are the days when some shall depart from the faith. . . . I think it's not just so much the disbelieving apostate, but more likely this permissiveness. They would give heed to the seducing spirits and doctrines of devils. It seems that the devil has a way of making very attractive the things that he proposes to mankind. (*Teachings of Spencer W. Kimball,* p. 267.)

Have some members of the Church, young and old, "departed from the faith" by ignoring or not practicing the standards of sexual morality advocated by the Savior, his Church, and its leaders? The scripture in Timothy also notes that in the last days many would forbid or perhaps see no need for marriage, and would have their consciences "seared with a hot iron."

I remember well the day when I was teaching at another university. We had a guest editor from one of the "men's magazines" come to campus and speak. While there, he urged the students to experiment with their sexual passions and inclinations. One student raised his hand and said he feared the guilt that would likely result because of his religious training. The editor replied that perhaps the student shouldn't listen to his conscience so much and do what would bring him pleasure and gratification. Surely we're seeing the fulfillment of prophecy in our own day.

As a Roaring Lion

It seems clear that Satan will work diligently in the last days trying to confuse people as to what is good and what is evil. Why would he do such a thing? He is a miserable person and seeks to make others miserable like himself. (See 2 Ne. 2:27.) He is the father of contention (see 3 Ne. 11:29) and works diligently on Latter-day Saints and others of "the elect" (see Matt. 24:24). He is at war with the Saints and has encompassed us about. (See D&C 76:29.) With his evil ways he will try to convince us he does not exist; he seeks to lull us into a state of pacification where we will say "all is well" so he can grasp us "with his awful chains." (See 2 Ne. 28:21–22.) His persuasive efforts will be very gradual, almost as if we are being led about with a light thread or flaxen cord. (See 2 Ne. 26:22.) He will stalk or seek after us much like a wild animal stalks its prey. Peter admonished, "Be sober, be vigilant; because your adversary the devil, as a roaring lion, walketh about, seeking whom he may devour." (1 Pet. 5:8.)

Satan also has a cunning plan by which he will try to destroy the work of God in the last days. (See D&C 10:12.) Part of this plan is to bombard the Saints of God and others with so much sexual stimuli that we will have a difficult time resisting the temptations surrounding us. I believe Satan is attacking on at least three fronts: (1) He promotes sexual relations both before and outside marriage; (2) He victimizes some with the terrible abuses of sex—child molestation, incest, rape, and other hideous sex acts; and (3) He promotes faulty views of sex through a constant barrage of information about sexuality, sex perversion, and sexually transmitted diseases, utilizing both the mainstream media and various forms of pornography. Once people are married, some will have a difficult time having a natural, normal sex relationship with a spouse partly because of what they have observed or have been taught regarding sexual matters while they were young.

How effective has Satan been with his campaign on these fronts? Very effective! Just watch TV talk shows nonstop for a week. What is the constant theme or topic of interest? Another evidence of Satan's effectiveness is this: President Kimball has observed that sexual incompatibility in marriage is the number one cause for divorce among Latter-day Saints. Likewise, Elder Hugh B. Brown noted that many LDS newlyweds are grossly ignorant on the subject of sex in marriage and many marriages have been harmed because of this misinformation. (See *Teachings of Spencer W. Kimball*, p. 312; Hugh B. Brown, *You and Your Marriage* [Salt Lake City: Bookcraft, 1960], p. 73.]

President Ezra Taft Benson clearly recognized these problems. He wrote:

The plaguing sin of this generation is sexual immorality. This, the Prophet Joseph said, would be the source of more temptations, more buffetings, and more difficulties for the elders of Israel than any other. (See *Journal of Discourses*, 8:55.)

President Joseph F. Smith said that sexual impurity would be one of the three dangers that would threaten the Church within—and so it does. (See *Gospel Doctrine*, pp. 312–13) It permeates our society. . . .

Never in this generation of ours have morals been so loose as now. Sex is all but deified, and yet at the same time, it is put before youth in its lowest, coarsest, and most debasing forms. The curtain of modesty has been torn aside. In play, book, movie, and television; in magazine story, picture, and advertisement, immorality stands out in all its vulgarity and rottenness. . . . We must be in the amoral and immoral world, it is true, but not of it. We must be able to drop off to sleep at night without having to first sing lullabies to our conscience. (*Teachings of Ezra Taft Benson*, pp. 277–78, 285.)

The Most Righteous Reserved for the Last Days

To face this onslaught from Satan, the Lord has reserved many of his most righteous spirits for our day.

In 1993 our family extended another generation, and Susan and I became grandparents. Ryan Douglas Barlow was born on February 28, to his parents Doug and Becky Barlow. As I held my little grandson in my arms for the first time, I was overwhelmed by the experience. I looked into his little eyes and wondered what he was thinking. And since that time I have worried not only for Ryan but also for all the other little children that are being born in these last days. What awaits them?

Our prophets have taught that the Lord has held these valiant spirits back until this time so that they can resist Satan and build the kingdom. For instance, President Benson declared:

"I know that the Lord is sending to the earth some of His very choicest spirits in this day when wickedness is most intense, when the gospel is upon the earth in all its fullness. I am sure He is sending to earth some of His very choicest spirits to help build up the kingdom to prove to those in the world that they should live the gospel, keep the commandments of God, and to be in the world and not partake of the sins of the world." (Ibid., pp. 495–96.)

If, indeed, the best spirits are reserved for the last days, and each generation is potentially more valiant that those preceding it, we now know why this must be so. Let us pray for Ryan Barlow and all the other valiant little children who will be born in these last days. Let us pray for Doug and Becky Barlow and all other parents who are charged to teach their children (D&C 68:25–28) so they will not be devoured by Satan, who will stalk and try to devour them "as a roaring lion." Let us pray for all the youth and Church leaders for their spiritual stewardships and callings in these turbulent last days.

Who will prepare and protect these young children as they grow up? Who will keep them from the grasp of Satan, who will undoubtedly tempt them in ways that previous generations have not known? I like the old saying, "If not me, who? If not now, when?" And just as important, how will we teach them? How can sexual abstinence before marriage be effectively taught so the Lord can "raise up . . . a pure people" that will serve him in righteousness prior to his second coming? (D&C 100:16.)

Chapter 2

THE MEDIA:
WHAT ARE THEY
TEACHING OUR YOUTH?

I believe that most Latter-day Saints have a true desire to teach morality and chastity to their youth. They understand the vital need for sexual abstinence before marriage and yearn to help their children have the blessings that come with obedience to God's commands.

I also believe that most parents mistakenly feel they (and the Church) are the major source of values for their children. At one time that may have been true. Unfortunately, with the increasing availability of television and other media, that's all changed.

If we're going to be able to give our children a proper understanding of sexual morality, we must know what we're competing against.

The Impact of Television

I had just finished a major writing project and was simply exhausted. So one Wednesday evening I decided to sit down with my family and watch television to unwind. We turned to one channel where a program, entitled something like "Graduation Night," depicted wealthy high-school seniors in California at their last school dance at an expensive hotel. The story seemed to intrigue my family as we watched the program and ate popcorn.

There was much about the program that was disturbing to me, but one plot line was particularly offensive. Almost every one of the senior boys of the graduating class had rented a room at the hotel for the evening to share with his date. One by one, these young men went up to their rooms with their dates. Surely, I thought, there would be some resistance from the young women. But there was none—not one word. Apparently it was just the thing to do. Go to the party. Have a drink or two. Eat. Dance. And then go upstairs and go to bed. What a routine!

As the program concluded I couldn't help but be astounded at how casual the whole episode had been. What a powerful message to young people viewing: Here's what to do at your high school graduation party! And there was not one word said by any student or teacher that such sexual behavior was inappropriate.

During the same week we had been bombarded with TV promotions for another program where Billy and Alyson would "finally get together" and decide to "go all the way." This program was widely viewed by many teenagers and young adults. The promos showed scintillating scenes of Billy and Alyson (whoever they were) in a bedroom embracing, followed by closeups of their clothing as it was removed and dropped to the floor.

I didn't care to watch the episode when Billy and Alyson would make the momentous decision to "get together" on evening television. But I was forming some opinions about the influences television and other forms of media were likely having on many young people in America.

Another program was even more offensive. The promotions teased that the two young lovers would finally decide to "go all the way." And decide they did. For thirty minutes we were given some of the most persuasive reasons I've heard on why eighteen year olds should start engaging in sexual relations before marriage. The show concluded with the big moment, complete with soft lighting and appealing music. I'm sure millions of youth were emotionally drawn to that subtle, powerful scene of immorality.

These examples are just the tip of the iceberg. On the average, TV viewers can watch at least nine thousand scenes of suggested sexual intercourse or innuendo during prime time annually. About 80 percent of these encounters are outside of marriage. ("Children Having Children," *Time*, Dec. 9, 1985, p. 81.) And those figures were generated in 1985! With the advent of MTV and cable television, those statistics surely have skyrocketed. I fear that in the future there will not only be more frequent sex but also more explicit sex during the prime-time viewing hours of 6:00 to 10:00 P.M. Such fare is already available in many European countries.

Greatest Influence in Lives of Young People?

Not long ago I was asked to speak to the faculty of Northridge Elementary School, which is near my home. During my speech we addressed a critical question: What is the greatest influence on young people today? Latter-day Saints and other family-oriented groups would like to believe that the family has the greatest influence. But what about the schools, public and private? Religious leaders and programs? Peers? The media? Government policies and practices? Of course, all of these areas in some way have impact on the lives of young people. But which one is most influential? Which has the greatest potential for either good or evil?

I had been reading a book entitled *Mandate for Change,* which includes chapters on the economy, health care, education, gangs and violence, the environment, welfare, and families. In investigating families, the authors made this observation:

"Today, nearly every household has a television set, and the average child spends as much time watching television as with parents and twice as much time as in school. While much research on the impact of television yields murky results, it is fairly well established that educational programming accelerates early learning and that televised violence exacerbates aggressive behavior."

Now note this:

"It is difficult to believe that the accumulated impact of such stimuli on marriage and families is insignificant. Average citizens certainly don't think so. In a 1991 survey, for example, only 2 percent of the respondents thought that television should have the greatest influence on children's values, but fully 56 percent believe that it does in fact *have the greatest influence—more than parents, teachers, and religious leaders combined.*" (See Elaine Cuilla Kamarack and William A. Galston, "A Progressive Family Policy for the 1990s," in *Mandate for Change,* ed. Will Marshall and Martin Schram [New York: Berkeley Books, 1993], pp. 153–78; italics added.)

That observation, if true, should be of interest not only to educators but others as well. And it has particular significance for young Latter-day Saints—where are they getting their sexual attitudes and practices? (In addition it should, if true, be a major concern of every LDS parent and Church leader!) Just think: *Some informed people now believe that the media is more influential in determining young people's values than parents, schools, and religious leaders combined!* That may not be so in all cases. I hope it is not in most Latter-day Saint homes. But is it possible we have all underestimated the power and influence of the media on our lives in forming attitudes and/or thoughts that eventually affect behavior?

The Fourth Learning Center

Anyone interested in learning more about the power of the media in our lives should read *Learn to Discern,* written by Robert G. DeMoss, Jr. (Grand Rapids, Michigan: Zondervan Publishing House, 1992). The author makes this important observation:

> There was a time in American history when the primary centers of learning were three in number: the school, the church, and the home. If your child was placed in a suitable school, if he was involved in a good church program, and given the fact that you supervised what was taking place at home, you could rest assured that your bases were covered.
>
> Today, however, there is a fourth center of learning: the world of popular entertainment personified in the chorus of "voices." These voices include the music industry, television and film industries, advertising, comic books, video games, and the news media. Even though they come wrapped in the innocent package called *entertainment,* all are capable of transmitting values, morals, ideologies, and attitudes about life in bigger-than-life terms. This combination of education and entertainment could be called *edutainment.* Recent technological breakthroughs—VCRs, Sony Walkman-type portable tape players, cable television, and consumer satellite dishes (all developed within the last two decades)—are now common household items that serve as the message bearers of this fourth center of learning. (Pp. 12–13.)

And what is DeMoss's assessment of the media's impact on the lives of contemporary children? "My experience working with children would indicate that they are frequently more tuned in to these voices than their classroom instruction, the church, or their home." (Ibid.)

Many Latter-day Saints may find this observation difficult to believe. But perhaps we should give it greater attention. Robert DeMoss believes that many parents and youth leaders are unaware of the tremendous influence the media has on us. He explains:

> I've noted three possible reasons for our extended nap. First, *there's widespread denial that a problem exists in popular entertainment.* Although we may concede that things are not perfect, we wrongly assume it can't be much worse than the era of Elvis shaking the nation with his pelvis. Second, *we'd like to believe that teens are unacquainted with the excesses of Hollywood,* so we hold on to a denial of any awareness. [Third,] for those of us alert enough to recognize that, in fact, a problem does exist and that our children are plugged into their culture, *we hope against hope that there is little impact upon behavior—a denial of influence.* Satisfied that there really isn't anything to be alarmed about, that our children somehow have a protective bubble which keeps them innocent, and that, in the event they do discover degrading entertainment imagery, no harm is done, we roll over for another snooze. (P. 10; italics added.)

The Power of the Media

Just how powerful is the media anyway? Of course no one really knows. Behavior doesn't come just from a single cause. That is, with human beings you cannot say that "A," all by itself, always causes "X." The behavior of human beings is usually multicausal. Many factors influence how human beings behave. In essence, "A, B, and C" cause "X." But how much of the influence is "A"? How much is "B"? How much is "C"? And what do we do when "X" is caused by "M" and "T"?

Whenever I have talked about the power of the media, many young people and/or adults just shrug their shoulders, suggesting that they do not believe that television and other forms of media have that much impact on our lives. If that is so, then why will advertisers pay $500,000 to $800,000 for a thirty-second television advertisement during the Super Bowl football game? The answer is simple: (1) the commercials are watched by millions of people worldwide; and (2) the viewers buy the products being promoted. Advertisers know the simple truth: trying to influence people through the media works!

Here are a few questions for you to consider the next time you wonder about the influence of the media (some of these are taken from a few advertisements from past years that you may still remember):

To which fast food restaurant should I go if I really believe I deserve "a break today"?

How do you spell "relief"?

Why, when we hear two non-words "Uh-Huh!" do we want to run to the store to buy Diet Pepsi? Do I "have the right one, Baby"? Why has this commercial made three attractive young women famous as the "Uh-Huh Girls"?

Why have certain beer advertisements tried to convince men that the best moments in life are not with their wife or children but up in the mountains drinking beer with a few buddies? As the voice-over in the commercial says, "It just doesn't get any better than this." (I only wish they would come back a few hours later when the men are all drunk and throwing up!)

Why can my young son, Brandon, repeat some commercials word for word? Why can we go shopping and he's able to tell me by brand name which cereal "we really should buy"?

Why does my young, emerging teenage daughter want to

drive the forty miles to certain stores with expensive clothing in Salt Lake City while good—but less known and less expensive brands—are available at the local mall?

For those who are a little older, I ask them to finish these sentences from cigarette commercials aired years ago: "Winston tastes good, like . . . " and "I'd walk a mile for . . ." and "I'd rather fight than . . . " I can still recall certain television (and even radio!) commercials from my youth some forty years ago. And from my teen years, why do I believe (still to this day!) that if I wear Old Spice shaving lotion I am more manly and attractive?

So what's the point of all this? If the media can sell us soap in thirty to sixty seconds (or now even fifteen seconds) it can also sell us a lifestyle.

Of course, all this isn't just my idea. Many others have recognized the problem. For example, one national Christian organization recently boycotted the advertisers of three television shows for the negative values those shows portrayed. The programs? "Married . . . with Children," "Roseanne," and "The Simpsons."

Messages from LDS Leaders

Our Church leaders have clearly expressed their concern about the effects of the media on the morality of Latter-day Saints.

President Ezra Taft Benson warned, "Too often television and movie screens shape our children's values." (*Teachings of Ezra Taft Benson,* p. 296.) He also noted:

> Now, what of the entertainment that is available to our young people today? Are you being undermined right in your homes through your television, radio, slick magazines, and rock music records? Much of the rock music is purposely designed to push immorality, narcotics, revolution, atheism, and nihilism through language that

often carries a double meaning and with which many parents are not familiar. . . . The devil-inspired destructive forces are present in our literature, in our art, in the movies, on the radio, in our dress, in our dances, on the television screen, and even in our modern so-called popular music. Satan uses many tools to weaken and destroy the home and the family, and especially our young people. Today, as never before, the devil's thrust is directed at you, our precious youth. (Ibid., p. 322.)

Undoubtedly sensing the power of the media, the First Presidency and Quorum of the Twelve of The Church of Jesus Christ of Latter-day Saints issued a pamphlet in 1990 entitled *For the Strength of Youth*. In it they counseled:

Whatever you read, listen to, or watch makes an impression on you. Public entertainment and the media can provide you with much positive experience. They can uplift and inspire you, teach you good and moral principles, and bring you closer to the beauty this world offers. But they can also make what is wrong and evil look normal, exciting, and acceptable.

Pornography is especially dangerous and addictive. Curious exploration of pornography can become a controlling habit leading to coarser material and to sexual transgression. If you continue to view pornography, your spirit will become desensitized, and your conscience will erode. Much harm comes from reading or viewing pornography. It causes thoughts within you that weaken your self-discipline.

Don't attend or participate in any form of entertainment, including concerts, movies, and videocassettes, that is vulgar, immoral, inappropriate, suggestive, or pornographic in any way. Movie ratings do not always accurately reflect offensive content. Don't be afraid to walk out of a movie, turn off a television set, or change a radio station if what's being presented does not meet your Heavenly Father's standards. And do not read books or magazines or look at pictures that are pornographic or that present immorality as acceptable.

In short, if you have any questions about whether a particular movie, book, or other form of entertainment is appropriate, don't see it, don't read it, don't participate. (*For the Strength of Youth,* pp. 11–12. Used by permission.)

It's not enough simply to teach our children positive values. We must also help them to avoid media that convey negative values. If we teach our children faithfully, but ignore the media they watch and listen to, we may well find that we are losing the war in the battle for their souls.

Chapter 3

ABSTINENCE TO AVOID
SEXUALLY TRANSMITTED DISEASES

We're having an epidemic of sexually transmitted diseases in the United States—and in many other nations of the world. President Ezra Taft Benson once observed: "The cause of so much social [venereal] disease and the reason it has become a 'killer-plague' is that so many, in their disregarding of God's truths, have abandoned the law of chastity. If we will live His law of virtue, we will destroy both immorality and its resultant diseases." (*Teachings of Ezra Taft Benson*, p. 279.)

Sexual Abstinence More Than a Moral Issue

The most critical reasons for sexual abstinence outside of marriage are moral and religious ones. As Latter-day Saints, we want to be morally clean because our Father in heaven has so commanded. To be sexually impure is a sin that can result in loss of the Spirit, loss of Church fellowship or membership, and ultimately even loss of exaltation.

But suppose for a moment there were no God in heaven (which there is!) and no true Church restored in the latter-days (which there is!). Suppose premarital sex were not a sin (which it is!), and men and women were just some higher form of animal life (which we are not!). Would there still be a rationale to teach and advocate sexual abstinence before marriage? The answer is an emphatic YES!

Could you or I go into any public school classroom today and make a strong, sound case for practicing sexual abstinence before marriage—without saying anything about morality? Or, could we attend any monthly public school board meeting and give a strong rationale for sexual abstinence before marriage as an option to the "condom" or "safe sex" approach (e.g., "if you are going to do it, be safe")? Could we make a case, if we had to, for sexual abstinence before marriage without mentioning God, religion, or sin? The answer, again, is yes, and some medical doctors have designed such a program to do so. It all has to do with sexually transmitted diseases.

Medical Institute for Sexual Health

In the early 1990s, a group of physicians in Austin, Texas, organized the Medical Institute for Sexual Health. Their goals include: (1) to warn and inform young single people about the deadly disease of AIDS, (2) to warn and inform young single people about twenty to thirty additional sexually transmitted diseases (STDs) that are growing in epidemic proportions, and (3) to warn and inform young single people (particularly women) about the infertility and even sterility that arises from these diseases.

These doctors are not part of the "safe sex" crowd. They argue that the only way to avoid the consequences of these diseases, including AIDS, *is through sexual abstinence before marriage*.

Dr. Joe S. McIlhaney, Jr., one of the founders of the Medical Institute for Sexual Health, has written a helpful and informative book called *Safe Sex: A Doctor Explains the Reality of AIDS and Other STDs* (Grand Rapids, Michigan: Baker Book House, 1991). In his book, Dr. McIlhaney documents the rise of sexually transmitted diseases during the past thirty years. He notes that prior to 1960, syphilis and gonorrhea were the only major sexually transmitted diseases. In 1976 chlamydia, once a rare disease associated with genital infection, became more common. Human immunodeficiency virus (HIV), the virus the leads to AIDS or acquired immune deficiency syndrome, was identified in the early 1980s. Between 1966 and 1984, herpes became more common and doctor office visits for treatment increased fifteen fold.

By 1990, more women were dying of human papillomavirus (5,000 a year), a genital disease, than were dying of AIDS. By 1990, syphilis was at a forty-year high. Pelvic inflammatory disease infected one million American women. Antibiotic resistant strains of gonorrhea were found in all fifty states. (See *Safe Sex,* p. 8.)

Dr. McIlhaney gives the following frightening statistics regarding sexually transmitted diseases (STDs):

• One in five Americans is now infected with a STD.
• 12 million people annually are new victims of a STD.
• 35 to 50 different forms of STDs now exist.
• Most STDs can be detected only with medical tests. (P. 10.)

As reported in a medical symposium on sexually transmitted diseases, "The situation is now nearly out of control." (*The Journal of the American Medical Association,* June 23/30, 1989, as quoted in *Safe Sex,* p. 12.)

There are dozens of different kinds of STDs, but here is a summary of those that occur most commonly:

AIDS

The most commonly known sexually transmitted disease today is AIDS (acquired immune deficiency syndrome), well known because of all the attention it has received from the media, schools, government, and even church organizations. AIDS is a viral infection caused by the human immunodeficiency virus (HIV). Technically, no one dies from the disease AIDS. HIV breaks down the immune system of the body, which then becomes susceptible to many other diseases. HIV is usually first contacted through sexual acts, either homo- or heterosexual, through use of dirty, "used" needles associated with drugs, or from tainted blood transfusions. HIV has been known to pass from patient to health-care workers (or vice versa) where exposed blood is present.

A person may be HIV positive for many months and even years and not know he or she has the disease, though it can usually be detected by a blood test in a matter of weeks. Usually, the HIV-positive person can expect some of the signs of AIDS within five to twelve years. He or she then often develops enlarged lymph nodes, usually in the back of the neck and under the arms. Some people have an intermittent fever, weight loss, occasional diarrhea, and candida mouth infections. Other signs of AIDS may include severe fatigue, persistent unexplained coughing, loss of memory, inability to think clearly, loss of judgment, and/or depression.

Once the immune system of the body has been sufficiently weakened, major problems develop and infections that would not normally occur invade the body. About 50 percent of AIDS victims die within a year after these developments. Within three years, the mortality rate is 90 percent. At the present time (1994) there is no known cure for AIDS, and, barring some miracle, all AIDS victims will eventually die from complications of the disease.

AIDS is spreading at an alarming rate in the U.S. The number infected with the disease doubles every 2.8 years, and the even more rapid spread of AIDS in other countries could be a sign of things to come. In some areas in Africa, for example, one in five women delivering babies are found to be HIV positive. Blood tests on all patients in a group of fifteen hospitals in Uganda during a one-week period found 42 percent were HIV positive. (Ibid., pp. 145–55.)

The U.S. Center for Disease Control estimates there are now approximately 350,000 AIDS cases in the U.S. Researchers estimate there are currently an additional 1.5 to 2 million persons who have the HIV virus in their blood but, as yet, show no symptoms of the disease. (Cox, *Human Intimacy,* p. 377.)

Human Papillomavirus (HPV) Infections

HPV infections cause "venereal warts" in the genital area in both men and women. Initially they only cause discomfort, but they are particularly dangerous for women, since they can lead to cancer of the cervix, vulva, or vagina.

The HPV infections are the most rapidly increasing sexually transmitted diseases. By 1990 this infection was killing more than 5,000 women annually, far more women than die each year from AIDS. It is now estimated that up to 30 percent of all sexually active women and men have this virus, with the percentage jumping to 46 percent among sexually active singles. Some 1.5 million new cases of HPV are reported in the United States each year. Some experts claim this infection has reached epidemic proportions. (*Safe Sex,* pp. 135–43.)

Chlamydia

Chlamydia is an infection that occurs in a woman's reproductive organs. It is contracted only by intercourse; when a woman gets the infection the first time, she has a 25 percent chance of becoming sterile. Each time she contracts the infection her chances of sterility increase 25 percent, until, after the fourth incident, she has a 100 percent chance of being sterile for the rest of her life. Chlamydia infects 20 to 40 percent of all sexually active singles; there are an estimated 3 to 5 million new infections every year. In addition to sterility, chlamydia can cause miscarriages and premature births, and it is a major cause of tubal pregnancies. It can also infect a baby at birth.

The most devastating thing about chlamydia for women is that it can develop into PID (pelvic inflammatory disease) which causes even more pain and expense. There are currently one million new cases of PID each year, which can result in sterility, hysterectomy, ectopic pregnancies, and even death. (Ibid., pp. 100–109.)

Herpes

Herpes is a virus that produces painful blisters and sores in and on the genitals in both males and females. Outbreaks can later appear anywhere on the body. There are 500,000 new cases of herpes reported each year, with the disease infecting from 30 to 40 percent of all sexually active singles. About 20 million Americans are now affected with herpes.

Since the often painful blisters do not appear for two weeks to several years after the first contact, an individual could have herpes and not know it—and can unknowingly pass it on to others.

Herpes is almost always contracted through sexual intercourse or other intimate physical contact. (Ibid., pp. 111–18.)

Gonorrhea

Gonorrhea is caused by bacteria that are almost always transmitted by sexual intercourse. Approximately 1.4 million new cases of gonorrhea are reported each year. And certain new forms of gonorrhea are proving to be resistant to antibiotics.

It is also a highly communicable disease. Just one sexual act with an infected partner brings a 40 percent chance of contracting the disease. To make matters worse, some 80 percent of both men and women infected with gonorrhea do not know it during the early stages, yet they can infect others. Gonorrhea can cause a pus-like discharge from the sex organs, a burning sensation during urination, a high fever, and skin rash. If untreated, or treated too late, gonorrhea can lead to other complications such as sterility for women. (Ibid., pp. 119–25.)

Syphilis

The incidence of syphilis has increased dramatically in recent years, much to the alarm of health officials. The incidence of syphilis is now at a forty-year high, with 130,000 new cases reported each year. Since the latter part of the 1980s, syphilis has increased 30 percent—but the increase among women is up 60 to 75 percent!

Over 50 percent of people who have intercourse just once with an infected partner will get syphilis. The first symptom is a lesion or sore that appears, usually within three weeks, at the place where the disease entered the body. Within six weeks to six months, additional symptoms appear: headache, fatigue, low-grade fever, skin rash, and enlarged lymph nodes. Infectious, oozing growths may develop on the skin. After the secondary syphilis stage has passed, a latent period follows, lasting anywhere from several months to twenty years.

The standard treatment for syphilis is penicillin, which is 100 percent effective in killing the disease. But if the disease is not diagnosed and treated early, during the latent period it will work its silent destruction in the victim's body day after day, year after year. The result can include irreversible damage to the bones, liver cells, heart valves, blood vessels, and the central nervous system. (Ibid., pp. 127–34.)

Hepatitis B

Hepatitis B is a virus that causes serious damage to the liver, often to the point of death. It can be transmitted through blood tranfusions, through contaminated intravenous needles, and through sexual intercourse. Like many of the other STDs noted, a person may be a carrier of this disease for many years and not know it. Some 300,000 new cases of hepatitis B are reported each year. If a pregnant woman has the disease she can pass it to her children; about half of all babies born with hepatitis B will develop cancer of the liver. Many others will have severe liver disease.

There is no known cure of hepatitis B but most people recover from the infection. Rest in a supportive environment is the best known care. Symptoms include jaundice, tiredness, and nausea. (Ibid., pp. 157–60.)

Vaginitis

The most common type of vaginitis is caused by a parasite that is spread only by sexual intercourse. It causes a vaginal discharge, a foul-smelling odor, and an itching that sometimes seems intolerable. Trichomoniasis vaginitis is now known to be one of the most common STDs in the world. It infects millions each year and is present in 10 to 20 percent of women of reproductive age. (Ibid., pp. 161–65.)

Avoiding the Epidemic

By now I hope it's clear that there are some real health concerns that come with sexual relations outside of marriage. We're in the middle of an epidemic of sexually transmitted diseases that can lead to body sores, foul odors, itching, cancer, liver damage, and much more, including death. If a person is sexually active outside of marriage, the odds are great that he or she will become another victim of the epidemic.

Certainly there are benefits that come from obeying the law of chastity, regardless of our motivation. For instance, we will receive real blessings if we abstain simply to avoid the epidemic! I hope the information just presented will help the youth of the

Church make an informed choice about the health consequences of sexual relations outside of marriage—and I hope they will choose to abstain.

But then I hope they will seek a higher motive—to live the law of chastity because they love God and want to please him. Such a motivation is the source of the greatest blessings.

Here is the conclusion Dr. McIlhaney reached in *Safe Sex:*

It bears repeating, I am convinced, that avoiding sex until marriage is the only wise course. In my desire to convince *you* of that fact, I have been greatly encouraged during the past two years. During this time I have had a large and ever-growing number of patients who are virgins or who have stopped having intercourse and plan not to resume sexual activity until marriage.

I know these women are going to experience happier and healthier lives than they would have otherwise. I am excited about this trend because I also believe that these women will gradually convince men that sex is safest and best enjoyed in marriage. . . .

I think this trend points to a new enlightenment whereby people are allowing their morality and their faith to direct them, instead of blindly responding to their physical urges and the pressuring of so-called friends.

Perhaps in the 1990s we will not only see new political freedom burst forth all over the world, but we will also see authentic sexual freedom reign in people's lives as they seek and find the joy of sex in marriage alone. (Ibid., pp. 96–97.)

President Ezra Taft Benson has also noted:

The world is already beginning to reap the consequences of their abandonment of any standards of morality. As just one example, the Secretary of the Department of

Health and Human Services in the United States warned that if a cure for AIDS is not quickly found, it could become a worldwide epidemic that "will dwarf such earlier medical disasters as the black plague, smallpox, and typhoid."

As the world seeks solutions for this disease, which began primarily through widespread homosexuality, they look everywhere but to the law of the Lord. There are numerous agencies, both public and private, trying to combat AIDS. They seek increased funding for research. They sponsor programs of education and information. They write bills aimed at protecting the innocent from infection. They set up treatment programs for those who have already become infected. These are important and necessary programs and we commend those efforts. But why is it we rarely hear anyone calling for a return to chastity, for a commitment to virtue and fidelity? (*Teachings of Ezra Taft Benson*, p. 410.)

Chapter 4

PERSPECTIVES ON
SELF-STIMULATION

When we speak of sexual abstinence outside marriage, we generally refer to an avoidance of fornication and adultery. But it is also important for us to avoid masturbation, or self-stimulation. While sexual sin with others is clearly of much greater consequence, it still is true that masturbation is a sin. Those who wish to enjoy the blessings of purity must be pure in all ways.

I have two primary cautions for parents, teachers, and youth leaders when they are discussing self-stimulation with young people. First, when discussing masturbation, we should not make it worse than it is. Though masturbation truly is a transgression, it is not as serious as fornication or adultery.

Second, we should not treat masturbation lightly, as something that is not a sin, or as a sin of no consequence. The potential harmful effects of self-stimulation are real. This is particularly true if it occurs over an extended period of time, is practiced frequently, and leads the participant in the path of social alienation or even sex addiction. Simply stated, self-stimulation can cause a person to seek sexual satisfaction alone, and, when added to mental fantasies, it can alienate him or her from others, making sexual fulfillment with a marriage partner less attractive. Imagination is often greater than reality.

Self-Stimulation a Common Practice

While different studies on self-stimulation or masturbation report various findings on the practice, almost all report that (1) the vast majority of young men (85–95 percent) engage in the practice at some point in their life, and (2) a lesser percentage, though a majority (50–75 percent), of young women do likewise. (For example, see Cox, *Human Intimacy,* p. 354.)

The Janus Report (1993) on sexual behavior found that 43 percent of the men and 18 percent of young women acknowledged masturbating at least "weekly." (Pp. 30–31.) And it is evidently occurring at a fairly early age. Seventy-two percent of the males and 44 percent of the females involved in the report had commenced the practice by age thirteen. Only about 5 percent of the males and 11 percent of the females in all age groups in this recent study indicated they had "Never" practiced self-stimulation. (P. 78.)

In his book *Christian Counseling: A Comprehensive Guide* (Waco, Texas: Word Books, 1980), Gary R. Collins notes: "Research studies generally conclude that about 95 percent of males, and a lower percentage (50 percent to 90 percent) of all females, have masturbated to the point of orgasm at least sometime in their lives. The frequency of masturbation declines following adolescence and after marriage, but it does not disappear. Apparently most married men and many married women continue to masturbate at times throughout their lives—and regular church attenders masturbate as much as the nonattenders." (P. 295.)

President Spencer W. Kimball has observed that "most youth come into contact early with masturbation" (*Miracle of Forgiveness* [Salt Lake City: Bookcraft, 1969], p. 77) and called the practice "a rather common indiscretion" (*Teachings of Spencer W. Kimball,* p. 282). Of course, he also pointed out that just because the practice was prevalent or common, it still was not acceptable.

Three Common Beliefs

It is evident to me that there are now, or have been, several common beliefs regarding self-stimulation:

Belief #1: Self-stimulation is a serious sexual sin, on the order of fornication, adultery, or homosexuality.

Belief #2: Self-stimulation causes physical and mental impairments.

Belief #3: Self-stimulation is a normal act in sexual development and should be neither encouraged nor discouraged.

Let's examine each of these beliefs in greater detail.

Common Belief #1: Self-stimulation is a serious sexual sin, on the order of fornication, adultery, or homosexuality.

The belief that self-stimulation is a serious sexual sin arises out of early Christian history and thought. Early Christians were influenced by Augustine's belief that concupiscence (strong desire)—and particularly concupiscence associated with sex—was the result of and the means of transmission of original sin. Therefore, Augustine taught, the only use of sex that could be justified was for the purposes of procreation. Later theologians rejected his teachings but taught instead that any sexual release outside marital intercourse, including masturbation, was wrong and a serious sin.

About 1750, S.A.D. Tissot of France wrote his *Onana, a Treatise on the Diseases Produced by Onanism,* and described the viciousness of "self-abuse," attributing most medical disorders—including consumption (a disease like tuberculosis), epileptic seizures, gonorrhea, and insanity—to the practice of masturbation. It was Tissot who introduced the fatuous and totally unscientific idea that the loss of one drop of seminal fluid causes more bodily damage and weakness than the loss of forty drops of blood. (See James Leslie McCary, *Human Sexuality* [New York: D. Van Nostrand Company, 1973], pp. 156–57.)

Various scriptures in the Old Testament have been used to condemn masturbation. The first is in Leviticus 15:16, which states, "And if any man's seed of copulation go out from him, then he shall wash all his flesh in water, and be unclean until the even." While some theologians believed this passage referred to masturbation, others believed it referred to an act of intercourse (see v. 18) or to nocturnal emissions. This latter group of theologians cited Leviticus 12:2 where a woman who just gave birth was pronounced "unclean" and had to go through seven days of purification. (See vv. 3–8.) Women were also deemed to be unclean for one day following sexual intercourse. (Lev. 15:18.) Women were, in addition, believed to be unclean for seven days after their menstrual cycles and likewise had to go through a purification process. (See Lev. 15:19–33.) (See Clifford and Joyce Penner, *The Gift of Sex* [Dallas: Word Publishers, 1981], p. 232.)

The primary passage of scripture used to condemn masturbation is Genesis 38:8–10, which is the story of Onan. He was commanded by the Lord to go to his deceased brother's widow and "raise up seed to thy brother." Onan knew that the children would not be his own, and after going to his brother's wife "he spilled it [his seed] on the ground, lest that he should give seed to his brother."

What Onan did has become known as "Onanism" in some religious circles, and it is considered by them to be a serious sexual sin. After all, they argue, the Lord slew Onan for his actions.

But the real cause of the Lord's anger was Onan's defiant refusal to have children with his brother's widow. First

Corinthians 3:16–17 has also been used in conjunction with Genesis 38:8–10 to imply that God will destroy those who defile the body, which is compared to a temple of God.

Common Belief #2: Self-stimulation causes physical and mental impairments.

In times past some authorities, including those in the medical profession, taught that self-stimulation or masturbation led to such dire results as mental insanity, physical impairment, and sometimes death. Few, if any, would entertain such beliefs today. Others have noted additional myths regarding the consequences of masturbation. These range from: "stooping shoulders to damage to the genitals, and have included insanity, paralysis, acne, excess growth of hair, loss of hair, epilepsy, fatigue, impotence, stomach ulcers, insomnia, weak eyes, skin rashes and loss of weight." (*Towards a Quaker View of Sex: An Essay by a Group of Friends* [London: Friends Home Service Committee, 1966], p. 18.)

Common Belief #3: Self-stimulation is a normal act in sexual development and should be neither encouraged nor discouraged.

Some believe that masturbation is a natural part of life. Following is a statement typical of those who advocate this belief:

"Masturbation is a perfectly normal, healthy act in boys and girls and in men and women, young and old. Nevertheless, it has long been a subject of great contention, and discussions of it are often rife with ignorance, misinformation, superstition, and shame. It is hence scarcely surprising that many people, especially the naive, come to believe that masturbation is an evil, abnormal, or at best, infantile practice." (McCary, *Human Sexuality*, p. 156.)

According to this way of thinking, the best method for parents, teachers, and religious leaders to discourage the act, if that is their goal, is to remain neutral. Do not pay excessive attention to it in the first place, and in time the youth will turn from the practice to other pursuits. (See Hugo G. Beigel, *Sex from A to Z: A Modern Approach to All Aspects of Human Sex Life* [New York: Stephen Daye Press, 1961], p. 209.)

Gospel Insights about Masturbation

Opposing these common beliefs about masturbation are gospel insights as given by our latter-day prophets. Self-stimulation is a sexual sin, and while it is not on the order of fornication, adultery, or homosexuality, still it can cause the loss of the Spirit, self-confidence, and focus in life.

President Spencer W. Kimball has noted:

"Many would-be authorities declare that it [masturbation] is natural and acceptable, and frequently young men I interview cite these advocates to justify their practice. To this we must respond that the world's norms in many areas—drinking, smoking, and sex experience generally, to mention only a few—depart increasingly from God's law. The Church has a different, higher norm." (*Miracle of Forgiveness,* p. 77.)

He also stated:

"Masturbation, a rather common indiscretion, is not approved of the Lord nor of his church, regardless of what may have been said by others whose 'norms' are lower. Latter-day Saints are urged to avoid this practice. Anyone fettered by this weakness should abandon the habit before he [or she] goes on a mission or receives the holy priesthood or goes in the temple for his blessings." (*Teachings of Spencer W. Kimball,* p. 282.)

On still another occasion, President Kimball observed:

All sex activity outside marriage is sin. The early apostles and prophets mention numerous sins that were reprehensible to them. Many of them were sexual sins—

adultery, being without natural affection, lustfulness, infidelity, incontinence, filthy communication, impurity, inordinate affection, fornication. They included all sexual relations outside marriage—petting, sex perversion, masturbation, and preoccupation with sex in one's thoughts and talking. Included are every hidden and secret sin and all unholy impure thoughts and practices. (Ibid., pp. 264–65.)

And finally, *A Parent's Guide,* published by the LDS Church in 1985, says: "The sin of masturbation occurs when a person stimulates his or her own sex organs for the purpose of sexual arousal. It is a perversion of the body's passions. When we pervert these passions and intentionally use them for selfish, immoral purposes, we become carnal. Masturbation is not physically necessary." (*A Parent's Guide* [Salt Lake City: The Church of Jesus Christ of Latter-day Saints, 1985], p. 37.)

Young people often want to know how serious masturbation is. President Kimball gives us the answer: "While we should not regard this weakness [self-stimulation] as the heinous sin which some other sexual practices are, it is of itself bad enough to require sincere repentance." (*Miracle of Forgiveness,* pp. 77–78.)

Reasons to Avoid Self-Stimulation

All sins have consequences. There are at least six consequences that come with masturbation:

• Loss of confidence before God.
• Loss of proper focus.
• Improper acceleration of sexual desire.
• Lessened control of sexual impulses.
• Possible habituation and addiction.
• Loss of the Spirit.

We should avoid all sin because we love God and desire to

please him. But in addition, we can legitimately desire to avoid the consequences of sin. Let's look at each of these, seeing them as reasons to avoid masturbation.

Reason #1: To keep a high level of confidence before God.

Latter-day revelation admonishes us to "let virtue garnish thy thoughts *unceasingly*" and the promise is, "then shall thy confidence wax strong in the presence of God." (D&C 121:45.) Those who are called to do the Lord's work in these latter days often face challenging situations where great confidence is needed. The Lord informs us that having virtuous thoughts helps bring and retain that confidence as it is needed.

Reason #2: To keep a proper focus.

Becoming unduly obsessed with sexual stimuli or pleasure can also cause one to lose the proper focus in life. The Apostle Paul admonished "whatsoever things are honest . . . are just . . . are pure . . . are lovely . . . of good report; if there be any virtue, and if there be any praise, *think on these things.*" (Philip. 4:8; italics added.) The Thirteenth Article of Faith urges us to "seek after" these things.

If we allow ourselves to continually think about or be obsessed with thoughts regarding inappropriate sexual behavior, our focus becomes distorted and we begin to think that that is the most important thing in life. The current media, in the form of advertising, movies, videos, and magazines, contribute to this perspective. Ancient scriptures note that thoughts usually precede acts: "As [a man] thinketh . . . so is he." (Prov. 23:7.) This affirms the modern wisdom that "we become what we think about." Focus in life, therefore, is critical because it involves choices we make constantly, every minute of every day.

Reason #3: To avoid the acceleration of sexual desire.

Almost all men and women have a natural and normal attraction for members of the opposite sex. That attraction is God-given and God-ordained, but it must be acted upon only within the bonds of marriage. Because of this strong attraction, young people (including Latter-day Saints) sometimes find their sexual impulses difficult to control before marriage. Yet the Lord expects us to do so and will help us in the process. (See 1 Ne. 3:7; 1 Cor. 10:13.)

Some have naively believed that self-stimulation before marriage will reduce sexual drive. In actuality, masturbation can accelerate the sexual desire, making it even stronger and more urgent.

Reason #4: To keep control of sexual impulses.

The admonition of the prophet Alma to "bridle all [our] passions" (Alma 38:12) was meant for both young and old, married and single. Sexual restraint is necessary throughout our entire lives and must begin when we are young and the desire is strong. Part of this restraint is the avoidance of self-stimulation.

Many single students at BYU are surprised when I suggest that some of their greatest sexual temptations will come not before marriage but afterward—with far more serious consequences. This is evidenced by the large number of husbands and wives in the United States who commit adultery. Unfortunately, even some Latter-day Saints who do not "bridle their passions" give in to this extremely serious sin. Learning to control or "bridle" our sexual impulses and passions, therefore, is something that is best learned in our youth (Alma 37:35), then continued throughout our entire lifetime.

Reason #5: To avoid possible habituation and addiction.

One of the most serious consequences of self-stimulation is that it can become a habit. From there it can also eventually lead to an addiction, which can lead a person from love, or genuine feelings, to lust, which is little more than physical gratification. Love usually focuses on other people. Lust often centers on one's self or on objects.

Regarding the gradual increase of lust within us, President Ezra Taft Benson noted:

Recently, a young man commented that if he quit reading books, watching television, seeing movies, reading newspapers and magazines, and going to school, there was a chance he might live a clean life. This explains, in large part, the extent to which the insidious evil of sexual promiscuity has spread, for the world treats this sin flippantly. These evil forces build up your lust and then fail to tell of the tragic consequences. In so many movies the hero is permitted to get away with crime so long as he can joke about it, or explain he was powerless to do anything, or else at the close of the movie show forth one minimal virtue that is supposed to cover over the grossest of sin. Many of our prominent national magazines pander to the baser side, but then try to cover themselves by including other articles, too. (*Teachings of Ezra Taft Benson,* pp. 409–10.)

Psychologists have noted a consistent pattern in sex addiction, where the addict gradually desires ever more explicit or deviant material—and eventually may end up acting out what he or she has seen.

The pattern begins with exposure to pornography or undesirable behavior. The next step is addiction, where the person simply "has to have it," and keeps going back to experience new sexual highs. Step three is escalation—previous sexual highs become more difficult to attain and addicts begin looking for more exotic forms of sexual behavior to bring them greater stimulation. The next step is desensitization—what was once initially shocking becomes routine and is no longer avoided. The final step involves the acting out of fantasies—sometimes even deviant or criminal ones. (See Kenneth Kantzer, "The Power of Porn,"

Christianity Today, Feb. 7, 1986, p. 18. Also see Victor B. Cline, "Another View: Pornography Effects, The State of the Art," in Victor B. Cline, ed., *Where Do You Draw the Line?* [Provo, Utah: BYU Press, 1974], pp. 203–44.)

Reason #6: To avoid the loss of the Spirit.

The Lord has clearly told us that the "Spirit shall not always strive with man" (D&C 1:33; Moses 8:17), and if we continue in sin without repentance, the Spirit will surely leave us. Paul wrote in Galatians 5:16–26 that if we participate in lustful acts we will not have the Spirit with us. Self-stimulation can be one of these acts of lust. Paul wrote: "Walk in the Spirit, and ye shall not fulfil the lust of the flesh. For the flesh lusteth against the Spirit, and the Spirit against the flesh: and these are contrary the one to the other: so that ye cannot do the things that ye would." (Gal. 5:16–17.) Among the "works of the flesh" identified are adultery, fornication, uncleanness, and lasciviousness [or excessive lust], and other uncontrolled and unruly acts. (See vv. 19–21.) Latter-day revelation also warns that lust can cause the loss of the Spirit. (See D&C 42:23; 63:16.)

For two years I had the opportunity to serve as a branch president at the Missionary Training Center in Provo. While in that position, I interviewed hundreds of missionaries, discussing their concerns and apprehensions about missionary work. Occasionally they would want to talk about feelings of lack of worthiness. Often they would talk about masturbation, wondering why it was so inappropriate.

The best answer I could give them was that as missionaries— and as God's children in any capacity—they needed the companionship of the Holy Ghost. Without that, they would fail.

For example, we read together the words of the Lord when he said, "Verily I say unto you, he that is ordained of me and sent forth to preach the word of truth by the Comforter, *in the Spirit of truth,* doth he preach it by the Spirit of truth or some other way? And if it be by some other way it is not of God." (D&C 50:17–18; italics added.)

Then we turned to various scriptures in modern revelation that help us understand how to gain and keep the Holy Ghost in our lives—or how to lose it. By having virtuous thoughts *unceasingly,* for instance, we are promised the *constant* companionship of the Holy Ghost. (See D&C 121:46.) And we read the words that say, "The Spirit shall be given unto you by the prayer of faith; *and if ye receive not the Spirit ye shall not teach.*" (D&C 42:14; italics added.)

I explained to the missionaries that self-stimulation truly was an act of lust and, as such, could result in our losing the Spirit. Obviously, other more serious sexual sins would do much the same with greater effectiveness and intensity.

On this subject President Ezra Taft Benson noted:

No sin is causing the loss of the Spirit of the Lord among our people more today than sexual promiscuity. It is causing our people to stumble, damning their growth, darkening their spiritual powers, and making them subject to other sins.

A reason for virtue—which includes personal chastity, clean thoughts and practices, and integrity—*is that we must have the Spirit and the power of God in our lives to do God's work.* Without that power and influence we are no better off than individuals in other organizations. That virtue shines through and will influence others toward a better life and cause nonmembers to inquire of our faith. (*Teachings of Ezra Taft Benson,* pp. 278–79; italics added.)

It is important not only for full-time missionaries to have the Spirit with them in their lives, but full-time members need that influence as well. In a great sermon, Nephi emphasized the need to be guided by the Spirit in all things: "Feast upon the words of Christ," he said, "for behold the words of Christ *will tell you all things what ye should do*. . . . Again I say unto you that if ye will enter in by the way, *and receive the Holy Ghost, it will show unto you all things what ye should do*." (2 Ne. 32:3, 5.)

The Lord desires to bless us with gifts and guidance all through our lives—but we can receive these things only if we have the Spirit. This great gift of the Holy Ghost comes to us only through righteous living and avoiding all acts of lust, through prayer, and by worthily partaking of the sacrament "that [we] may always have his Spirit to be with [us]." (D&C 20:77.)

Self-stimulation and other acts of lust serve to drive the Spirit away. Repentance and worthiness help to bring the Spirit back.

Stopping the Habit

Latter-day Saints who become involved in self-stimulation and want to stop the habit should realize that the Lord and the gospel can help them in a variety of ways.

First, the Lord has promised he will assist with *any* weakness we have. He has declared, "My grace is sufficient for all men [and women] that humble themselves before me; for if they humble themselves before me, and have faith in me, then will I make weak things become strong unto them." (Eth. 12:27.)

Second, the sexual stimuli available in magazines, books, videos, television, movies, and other media are so strong that many people believe they are not able to resist the temptation to masturbate. But we must remember that the Lord has promised he will not allow Satan to tempt us beyond our ability to resist. This is because "with the temptation [the Lord will] also make a way to escape, that ye may be able to bear it." (1 Cor. 10:13.) In this case, the escape will often come as he helps us learn to avoid inappropriate media in the first place. It is comforting to know that the redemptive powers of Christ are always greater than the tempting powers of Satan—and we can choose who will be our master.

Third, those trying to stop the habit should realize that Christ really wants to help us win the moral battles we face in life. Nephi testified we should rely "wholly upon the merits of him who is *mighty to save*. Wherefore, ye must press forward with a steadfastness in Christ, having a perfect brightness of hope, and a love of God and of all men. Wherefore, if ye shall press forward, *feasting upon the word of Christ* [reading scriptures, listening to prophets, and following the Holy Ghost], and endure to the end, behold, thus saith the Father: Ye shall have eternal life." (2 Ne. 31:19–20; italics added.)

Fourth, latter-day revelation declares: "Pray always, that you may come off conqueror; yea, that you may conquer Satan, and that you may escape the hands of the servants of Satan that do uphold his work." (D&C 10:5.) Prayer can both help prevent the habit and overcome it if it has found place in one's life.

Fifth, those who can learn to control their thoughts can also control their deeds, including masturbation. Christian writer Norman Vincent Peale said, "Change your thoughts and you change your world." As in all things, Jesus Christ should be our model. The Lord said to Isaiah, "For my thoughts are not your thoughts, neither are your ways my ways, saith the Lord. For as the heavens are higher than the earth, so are my ways higher than your ways, and my thoughts than your thoughts." (Isa. 55:8–9.)

Sixth, scripture, both ancient and modern, encourages us to forget "those things which are behind" (Philip. 3:13) and "let not [our] minds turn back" (D&C 67:14). Not dwelling on past sins, mistakes, or inability to control the habit will be helpful in overcoming it.

Seventh, we should remember that *all* our sins will not only be forgiven but also forgotten by the Lord if we truly repent of them. "Behold, he who has repented of his sins, the same is forgiven, and I, the Lord, remember them no more." (D&C 58:42.) Sometimes openly communicating the problem with your bishop or stake president may help diffuse its destructive impact and set your feet more firmly on the path to repentance.

For Those Who Need Help

Dr. David Seamons is an LDS psychologist who has also served many years as a bishop, a stake president, and a regional representative. He has counseled numerous youth on masturbation both in his private practice and in his church callings. Over the years, Elder Seamons has shared some of his ideas with other LDS church leaders who similarly interact and counsel with LDS youth. Here are some of his valuable insights and suggestions on this subject.

Scriptural Perspectives

1. We have been sent here to this earth to be tried and tested. This is part of the plan. (See Abr. 3:24–26.)

2. Sins of the flesh are the most common because we never had a physical body before coming to mortality, and therefore we are inexperienced on how to curb our desires or control our passions. (See Gal. 5:16–26.)

3. The law of opposition mandates that everything created for good brings eternal happiness. Or it can be misused, leading to eternal unhappiness. (See 2 Ne. 2:11, 15.)

4. With regard to masturbation, it does not matter whether the world considers it a "normal" behavior or not. The Lord's prophets have counseled that "all" passions and desires are to be subject to self-discipline and control. (See Alma 38:12.)

Steps to Overcoming a Habit of Masturbation

Start by making a plan—you must be proactive! Fortify yourself with an arsenal of alternatives and options designed to prevent, distract, or interrupt sexual impulses which may lead to masturbation.

A plan to overcome a masturbation habit ought to focus on breaking the cycle of behavior. That cycle looks like this:

Stimulus leads to . . .

   Thoughts, which lead to . . .

      Emotions, which lead to . . .

         Behavior, which leads to a desire for additional stimulus.

Let me describe each of these elements in the cycle—and suggest how one can deal with them.

1. *Stimulus.* A stimulus generally evokes and precedes a thought. Stimuli can be external, coming from outside of ourselves, or internal, already programmed into the mind's computer by previous experiences.

Breaking the cycle: Avoid stimuli that excite or arouse sensual impulses, such as movies, videos, television shows, music, pornography, and so forth. If sexually related stimuli are avoided, thoughts are much easier to control.

2. *Thoughts.* We are taught, "As [a man] thinketh in his heart, so is he." (Prov. 23:7.) Thoughts generally follow a stimulus. You may not always be able to control what comes into your mind, but you can learn to control that which you dwell on or continue to think about.

Breaking the cycle: If you find that your thoughts are sexually arousing, you must immediately stop them. Distraction of undesired thoughts becomes one of the tools of a well-disciplined mind. Replace inappropriate thoughts with positive and wholesome ones. This can be done by praying out loud, reading the scriptures out loud, reading other good books out loud, singing uplifting songs, reciting poetry out loud, and so forth.

Another strategy found helpful by some has been to take the current sexual fantasy and exchange it for a more wholesome fantasy, one you've already selected and prepared. Such wholesome fantasies might include a detailed fantasy in which you see yourself successfully overcoming this challenge; or you can fantasize yourself as a successful and happy husband or wife, father or mother; or you can see yourself succeeding as president of the United States, a famous athlete, or an astronaut walking on the moon. The idea is to distract yourself and to replace inappropriate thoughts or fantasies with appropriate ones.

3. *Emotions.* One of the strongest of all human emotions is sexual arousal. Although arousal also involves physiological changes, the psychological mindset that produces emotions of desire is even more important. In fact, if our emotions are under control, physical arousal usually will not occur.

Breaking the cycle: If you have become emotionally aroused, changing your thoughts may not be enough. Try to assess how you are feeling. Take a paper and pencil and write in a column your feelings at that moment (i.e., confused, discouraged, frustrated, excited, hopeless, and so forth). Then write in an opposing column how you would like to be feeling (i.e., clarity of thought, encouraged, peaceful, under control, full of hope, and so forth). The identification of current and desired feelings can provide an additional distraction that will allow

you to regroup, refocus, and avoid a potential masturbation episode.

4. *Behavior:* If you have not been successful in controlling your stimuli, thoughts, or emotions, physiological and emotional arousal will usually occur. Your body
will begin to expect some form of release or satisfaction.
This is when the temptation to masturbate can become a
real challenge.

Breaking the cycle: It now becomes necessary to get
up and *do* something. If trying to control your thoughts
and emotions has not worked, get up and go talk to
someone—a roommate, a friend, or a family member. You
need not tell them what you're struggling with, just talk
about anything uplifting. Physical exercise can be helpful.
Some have found success in taking a *cold* shower. Whatever you do, exert energy as a form of distraction. Remember that sexual arousal is mainly psychological in nature. If
you can change the stimulus, thought patterns, and emotions, the physiological element of arousal will disappear.

In summary, masturbation is a result of a consistent
sequence of events: first stimuli, then thoughts, then
emotions, and finally behavior. It would be helpful if you
could identify the way that sequence works in your own
life, and then break the cycle however possible.

Generally, masturbation occurs in predictable circumstances. Perhaps the most common times for masturbation temptations are late at night while preparing
to sleep, early in the morning while awakening, or while
in the bath or shower. Individuals could observe the
cycle that most affects them and make a plan to avoid
succumbing to temptation during these critical periods.
For example, prior to going to bed, they could have a
light on near the bed and read from the scriptures until

going to sleep. In the morning, they could avoid lying in bed and get up immediately after awaking and go about the day's activities. They could also be on alert for problems that may occur during daytime naps. It is also helpful to avoid spending excessive time in the bathroom while showering or bathing. A constant fortification of personal prayer, scripture reading, fasting, and service to others provides a shield of protection against these temptations. (Note: It has been found that talking excessively about this problem with peers or friends can perpetuate it rather than help in overcoming it.)

We must also remember that males will sometimes awaken with an erection, which should be considered normal. Some may also have an erection during the night as part of the sleep cycle. Nocturnal emissions ("wet dreams") are nature's way of emptying the prostate gland. This may occur during the sleep stage or while waking up, and it is not considered masturbation unless the individual consciously adds stimulation to the process.

For those who have earnestly tried all of the above with little or no results, do not give up hope. The problem of masturbation can become an addiction, but it is one that can be overcome, though in some cases professional counseling may be needed. This may particularly be the case when the inability to conquer masturbation is linked with depression or other psychological or physiological problems. (Dr. David T. Seamons, *Helping LDS Youth Overcome Masturbation,* excerpts from unpublished manuscript. Used by permission.)

A Caution for Those with Little Children

Before we leave this important subject, I'd like to give a caution to LDS parents with young children. We should remember that "little children are whole, for they are not capable of committing sin." (Moro. 8:8.) Further, we read:

"Little children need no repentance. . . . Little children are alive in Christ, even from the foundation of the world. . . . Wherefore, I love little children with a perfect love; and they are all alike and partakers of salvation. . . . Little children cannot repent; wherefore, it is awful wickedness to deny the pure mercies of God unto them, for they are all alive in him because of his mercy." (Moro. 8:11–12, 17, 19.) Because of these truths, parents should be encouraged not to overreact if a small child becomes involved in self-stimulation in some way.

Dr. Lynn Scoresby, an LDS psychologist, has noted that self-stimulation is common in young boys and girls and often has no sexual overtones or intent. He observed:

Most children stimulate their genitals, usually before going to sleep when they turn on their stomachs and place their hands between their legs, or during bathing, or diaper changing. Occasionally, children will engage in prolonged stimulation. Girls, for example, will stimulate themselves with their hands or the corner of the bed or some other piece of furniture. Boys will stimulate themselves while going to the bathroom or while outside playing. In most cases with children under eight years of age, it is advisable simply to remove their hands without saying anything, or if that does not succeed, to talk with them about not touching themselves. Usually, the less said and done, the better, because too much attention could aggravate a situation that would have soon disappeared on its own. (*Bringing Up Moral Children* [Salt Lake City: Deseret Book Co., 1989], p. 105.)

Chapter 5

IT MATTERS *HOW* WE TEACH SEXUAL ABSTINENCE

It's clear from modern-day revelation that Latter-day Saint parents and Church leaders have the responsibility to teach young people gospel truths. (See D&C 68:25–28 and 93:41–42, 47–48, 50.) That certainly includes the importance of sexual abstinence before marriage and sexual fidelity after marriage.

How do we teach these vital truths about sexual morality? Our methods matter. One day our children are single, when sexual relations are taboo; the next day they are married, and sex is suddenly both acceptable and important. Will our teachings help them to stay morally clean during their growing years—and at the same time help them to make the transition to healthy married life? Or will we somehow convey false understandings that will linger with them throughout their lives?

The Most Important Things in Our Lives

Elder Bruce R. McConkie is well remembered for his comprehensive knowledge of the gospel and the valiant testimony of Christ that he bore. Considering all he knew and taught about the restored gospel, I have always been impressed with an observation he made regarding marriage. He said:

"The most important things that any member of The Church of Jesus Christ of Latter-day Saints ever does in this world are: (1) To marry the right person, in the right place, by the right authority, and (2) to keep the covenant made in connection with this holy and perfect order of matrimony." (*Mormon Doctrine*, 2nd ed. [Salt Lake City: Bookcraft, 1966], p. 118.)

That being so, and I truly believe it is, how we teach our children and prepare them for temple marriage is of vital importance. In this age of easy divorce, we must seek to help them establish a marriage that will last for eternity.

What does this have to do with the teaching of sexual morality before marriage?

Some years ago President Spencer W. Kimball noted: "If you study the divorces, as we have had to do in these past years, you will find there are one, two, three, four reasons. Generally sex is the first. They did not get along sexually. They may not say that in the court. They may not even tell that to their attorneys, but that is the reason." (*Teachings of Spencer W. Kimball*, p. 312.)

More than thirty years ago Elder Hugh B. Brown similarly observed: "Many [LDS] marriages have been wrecked on the dangerous rocks of ignorant and debased sex behavior, both before and after marriage. Gross ignorance on the part of newlyweds on the subject of the proper place and functioning of sex results in much unhappiness and many broken homes. Thousands of young people come to the marriage altar almost illiterate insofar as this basic and fundamental function is concerned." (*You and Your Marriage*, p. 73.)

I often read these quotes to my students at BYU and then ask why it is that so many LDS couples have a problem, as President Kimball noted, with sexual compatibility in their marriages. Why is there, as Elder Brown observed, "gross igno-rance on the part of newlyweds on the . . . proper place and functions of sex"? The students respond with answers that are interesting, revealing, and sometimes startling.

Some students say we don't talk much about sex in our homes. When we do, the mothers usually talk to the daughters and the fathers talk to the sons. Others suggest that those who practice sexual abstinence before marriage begin their married life relatively ignorant and uninformed in regard to sexual mat-ters. And some emphasize that how we are taught about sex while we are young either helps or hinders the transition into marriage. It appears that some teachers or parents, though well meaning, have approached the topic of sexuality in ways that do damage as well as good. Here are some approaches that concern me:

COMPARISONS AND ANALOGIES. Comparing some-thing known and understood with something less known is a teaching technique used by the Lord. (See D&C 88:46, 51.) Some parents and teachers in the Church have used the same approach in teaching chastity to youth, but their comparisons are not always appropriate. For example, many youth have seen the analogy of the crushed rose: the person who has remained sexu-ally pure is compared to a beautiful rose, while the person who has sinned sexually is compared to a crushed rose, whose beauty and desirability no longer exist. Similar lessons have been given using chewed-up bubble gum and handfuls of cake topped with icing passed from one class member to another (the cake is desir-able and looks delicious, but when it's been handled, no one wants it).

Many of these teaching techniques arose years ago when rel-atively few LDS youth were sexually indiscreet. It was an attempt to "keep the pure pure." But real care must be exercised in using such analogies at the present—teachers will likely have one or more young people in their classes who have already been immoral.

What does it feel like to be a "crushed rose" anyway?

Another technique used widely in teaching sexual abstinence involves a board, a hammer, and a nail. The nail is hammered in the board, representing sin, and then the nail is pulled, representing repentance. The hole left in the board supposedly represents lost virtue that can never be regained. What would this demonstration mean to a young man or woman who had recently engaged in intimate relationships? Would it give them hope to repent? Or despair?

EXCESSIVE GUILT. Once young people are properly counseled, cautioned, or warned about their sexual sins, we should not use excessive guilt as a means to turn them away from their errant behavior. Guilt is excessive when it causes one to feel the sinful behavior is even worse than is truly the case. If we teach young people to pray, the Holy Ghost and the Light of Christ will likely act as the "buffeter" to turn them to the paths of righteousness. The use of excessive guilt would also be questionable with mentally unstable young men and women, particularly when it comes to dealing with self-stimulation or masturbation. Excessive guilt with such individuals may just prolong the behavior. They may feel that because they have sinned there is no hope, so they may as well keep on sinning.

An opposite problem is feeling no guilt. Guilt is one of God's gifts to help us come to repentance. Unfortunately, some people don't feel guilt for their sins. The scriptures warn that in the last days many would have a conscience "seared with a hot iron." This implies they would fail to listen to their conscience as a guide for proper moral behavior, including sexual behavior. Paul noted some people would also "kick against the pricks" of conscience, comparing us and the Lord to a man driving an ox with a long crooked stick. (See Acts 9:5; 26:14; D&C 121:38.)

Teachers, leaders, and parents need to take care that they don't put too much guilt on their youth—or too little.

EXCESSIVE FEAR. Scriptures, both ancient and modern, teach that we should "fear the Lord." (For instance, there are more than sixty references to "Fear of God" in the Topical Guide in the Bible.) We read in Psalms 2:11 the injunction to "serve the Lord with fear and rejoice with trembling"; and in Psalms 112:1 we read the promise, "Blessed is the man that feareth the Lord."

But "fear" in the scriptures often does not mean "afraid." In the footnotes fear is often used interchangeably with obedience, reverence, and worship. We should be respectful with the Lord; we should be reverent. But he does not want the righteous to be afraid of him.

Is fear of punishment or God's anger an effective means of teaching sexual abstinence? Perhaps some fear of the consequences of sin is necessary. But excessive fear may make sex even more forbidden and therefore more intriguing and inviting for young people. Excessive fear should be used with caution when teaching sexual abstinence.

I remember attending an unusual stake Aaronic priesthood meeting when I was a young boy. The meeting was on sexual purity and one of the older leaders used "fear" as a motivator in his talk. He described in detail the depths of a burning hell that awaited the fornicator and the adulterer. He rehearsed what it would be like to stand before the Lord as an unclean, unrepentant sinner. He described a giant movie screen where all our sins during mortality would be reviewed, not only by us and the Lord but also by anyone else who wanted to watch. He had all of us shivering in our seats. But in hindsight I wonder if his "fear" tactics really were effective—and I wonder if his sermon had any harmful effects in later marriages of those who heard him.

As I noted concerning the AIDS crisis during the past

decade, fear has not been an effective deterrent to sexual promiscuity. In fact, as I discussed earlier, some feel that all the attention devoted to AIDS, without any guidelines for behavior, may have actually contributed to the increase of sexual behavior before marriage.

ONCE IMPURE, ALWAYS IMPURE. I once had two teachers who approached the topic of sexual abstinence in very different ways. One teacher implied that once we have "lost our virtue" it cannot ever be totally regained. He cited the parable of the prodigal son and suggested that though he repented and was forgiven, he would never attain the stature and degree of exaltation received by the son who remained faithful. (See Luke 15:11–32.)

The second teacher suggested that, through genuine repentance, purity and virtue could be regained—completely.

I personally feel there is real spiritual danger in implying to young people that virtue and purity cannot be regained once lost. While many young people today wrongly think the process is easy and simple, they must know that the door is open for a complete return. If young couples truly believe that virtue has been lost with no way to regain it, they may become unduly discouraged. In their discouragement, they may turn from the Savior (who, they've been falsely taught, cannot fully save them) and follow Satan even more. In an effort to emphasize sexual morality, we must not place limits on the depth, breadth, or power of the atonement of Jesus Christ. We must not say that he will not forgive and heal and make new when he has invited all to come to him to receive these very blessings. (See 3 Ne. 9:13–14; Alma 5:33–35; 42:27.)

This testimony given by President Benson should help us all to understand this truth:

> Yes, one can repent of moral transgression. The miracle of forgiveness is real, and true repentance is accepted of

the Lord. But it is not pleasing to the Lord to sow one's wild oats, to engage in sexual transgression of any nature and then expect that planned confession and quick repentance will satisfy the Lord. . . . The Prophet Joseph Smith taught: "God does not look on sin with allowance, but when men have sinned, there must be allowance made for them" ([*Teachings of the Prophet Joseph Smith*], pp. 240–41). That is another way of saying God loves the sinner, but condemns the sin. . . .

Remember that through proper repentance, *you can become clean again.* For those who pay the price required by true repentance, the promise is sure. *You can be clean again.* The despair can be lifted. The sweet peace of forgiveness will flow into your lives. In this dispensation the Lord spoke with clarity when he said, "Behold, he who has repented of his sins, the same is forgiven, and I, the Lord, remember them no more" (D&C 58:42). (*Teachings of Ezra Taft Benson,* pp. 70, 284; italics added.)

BETTER DEAD THAN IMMORAL. Once I counseled with a BYU student in her middle twenties. She had just broken up with her fiancé after having sexual relations with him. She was very distraught, questioning whether or not she would ever find anyone else to marry. She wondered out loud if life was still worth living; after much discussion she admitted she had seriously considered taking her own life.

I told her I understood the seriousness of the offense, as well as the pain of her broken heart, but I assured her that the pain would pass, and she could find forgiveness for the sin through repentance. Taking her own life would only make things worse. (I also referred her to the campus counseling center, where she could get help with her suicidal thoughts.)

She wasn't sure she accepted my argument. She was a convert

to the Church, and she'd been taught a lesson on morality shortly after her conversion. Her teacher had told her about an LDS father whose son was about to leave home. The father had warned the young man about the perils of the world, and had informed his son that he (the father) would rather see his son return home dead in a coffin than to return home sexually impure.

If it is better to be dead than impure, this young woman said, then I might as well take my own life.

I tried to convince her otherwise, and once again bore testimony of the possibility of repentance and forgiveness.

I fear that those who tell such stories to young people do them a real disservice. They eliminate the possibility of repentance and, in the process, discount the power of the Savior and his atonement.

EMOTIONAL VOYEURISM. Youth leaders have the opportunity to teach sexual morality during interviews. But in doing so, they should use careful discretion. In the current temple recommend book, bishops are discouraged from asking personal questions regarding intimate sexual behavior between a husband and a wife. Perhaps that same discretion should be used with youth and young adults, particularly when men are interviewing young women. I have sat on several disciplinary counsels in the Church and felt the questioning by a few, perhaps for reasons of personal curiosity, sometimes went far beyond propriety. LDS bishops and stake presidents have a spiritual mandate to know enough of the details to help the young woman or young man repent of the sins. But care should be used by them and others not to ask detailed or unnecessary questions that could add additional pain or embarrassment to young members. And always, confidences should be maintained "that the church may not speak reproachfully of him or her." (D&C 42:92.)

SEX IS DIRTY AND EVIL. You may have heard the admonition: "Sex is something dirty and evil; save it for someone you love." While we might smile at the paradox of such a statement, we also realize that this is often the message we give young Latter-day Saints regarding sex and sexual restraint. If such is the message with which we constantly bombard our young people, it is little wonder that many Latter-day Saints, as President Kimball observed, later have sexual problems in their marriages.

To make matters worse, the message that "sex is evil and dirty" is not conveyed only by insensitive teachers. It is communicated almost daily by the media. You don't believe it? Do an experiment. For just two or three days review the local newspaper or watch the nightly newscasts, national or local. Make careful notes of any incident regarding sexuality and write down how it happened. Was it incest? Child molestation? Rape? Murder and/or violence? Homosexuality? Child sexual exploitation by a youth or church leader? Listen to the jokes told by comedians. Watch the TV talk shows. When you have finished your experiment, see if what you have seen and heard has left you with any good feelings about sex.

Historically, some religious leaders have also implied that sex was just a necessary evil by which children were conceived. Some members of our Church may share similar views.

Is sex really that evil? Is God using a devilish means to accomplish divine purposes? Could he not have devised some other method so that sex, with all its supposed evils, could have been avoided by mortals? President Kimball answered this question by saying:

> When the Lord organized his world and established his policies, he could have filled the earth with physical bodies in some other way than that which he designed— perhaps some kind of an incubator process. But it seems that merely filling the earth with humans was not the great objective of our Lord. In order to properly people

the world it was necessary that every child born into this world should have two parents, a father and a mother, to teach him, to train him, to love him, that that child should be made aware of what was expected of him.

Rather than devise some incubator process for bringing children into this world, God created the human bodies. (Gen. 1:27–28.) . . . [His plan] required both a man and woman to reproduce through sexual relations and to also care for, rear, and teach the child gospel truths once he/she was born. . . . This process of reproduction was designed before this world was organized: "Wherefore, it is lawful that he [man] should have one wife, and they twain shall be one flesh [or relate sexually], and all this that the earth might answer the end of its creation; And that it might be filled with the measure of man, according to his creation before the world was made." (D&C 49:16–17.) ("Marriage Is Honorable," *Speeches of the Year: BYU Devotional and Ten-Stake Fireside Addresses, 1973* [Provo, Utah: BYU Press, 1974], p. 256.)

Elder Parley P. Pratt similarly noted:

The fact is, God made man, male and female; he planted in their bosoms those affections which are calculated to promote their happiness and union. That by that union they might fulfill the first and great commandment, viz: "To multiply and replenish the earth, and subdue it." From this union of affection, springs all the other relationships, social joys and affections diffused through every branch of human existence. And were it not for this, earth would be a desert wild, an uncultivated wilderness. (*Writings of Parley Parker Pratt,* ed. Parker Pratt Robison [Salt Lake City: Parker Pratt Robinson, 1952], pp. 53–54.)

From these scriptures and insights, it is clear that the sexual relationship between a husband and a wife is of divine origin and should serve divine purposes. Without it, the earth would be wasted and the purposes of God would be thwarted. Such is the importance of sex for married Latter-day Saints. We should, therefore, heed the warning of Mormon: "Wherefore, take heed, my beloved brethren, that ye do not judge that which is evil to be of God, *or that which is good and of God to be of the devil.*" (Moro. 7:14; italics added.)

Sex Has a Divine Origin and Purpose in Marriage

It's clear that there are questionable ways to approach and teach about sexuality—but how might it be done appropriately and effectively? How can Latter-day Saint parents, teachers, and youth leaders approach the topic in a way that (1) will encourage sexual abstinence before marriage, and (2) prepare young people for future sexual relations in marriage? The prophets of the Lord and other Church leaders give us an approach that can help.

The approach is this: We should teach that sexual relations are good and wholesome and pure in the right time and place (meaning, in marriage). Knowing that reserving sex for marriage brings the greatest happiness, a loving Heavenly Father has commanded his children to wait for the bonds of marriage to enjoy the intimacy of sex relations.

President Kimball has written: "Husband and wife . . . are authorized, in fact they are commanded, to have proper sex when they are properly married for time and eternity. That does not mean that we need to go to great extremes. That does not mean that woman is the servant of her husband. It does not mean that any man has a right to demand sex anytime that he might want it. He should be reasonable and understanding and it should be a general program between the two, so they understand and everybody is happy about it." (*Teachings of Spencer W. Kimball,* p. 312.)

President Kimball also said: "In the context of lawful marriage, the intimacy of sexual relations is right and divinely approved. There is nothing unholy or degrading about sexuality in itself, for by that means men and women join in a process of creation and in an expression of love." (Ibid., p. 311.)

In a general conference address, President Kimball quoted Billy Graham as saying: "The Bible celebrates sex and its proper use, presenting it as God-created, God-ordained, God-blessed. It makes plain that God himself implanted the physical magnetism between the sexes for two reasons: for the propagation of the human race, and for the expression of that kind of love between man and wife that makes for true oneness. His command to the first man and woman to be 'one flesh' was as important as his command to 'be fruitful and multiply.'" ("Guidelines to Carry Forth the Work of God in Cleanliness," *Ensign*, May 1974, p. 7.)

President Benson gave us similar teachings. He said: "The natural [sexual] desire for men and women to be together is from God. But such association is bounded by His laws. Those things properly reserved for marriage, when taken within the bonds of marriage, are right and pleasing before God and fulfill the commandment to multiply and replenish the earth. But those same things when taken outside the bonds of marriage are a curse." (*Teachings of Ezra Taft Benson*, p. 279.)

President Benson also observed: "God created sex, but not for self-indulgence. Men are not animals, left only to their instincts and self-indulgence. We are offspring of God. God Himself has set the boundaries of this sacred act. Sex outside of marriage is wrong. Every form of homosexuality is wrong. Through His Prophets He has declared and reiterated, 'Thou shalt not commit adultery.'" (Ibid., p. 280.)

Finally, President Benson said, "Sex was created and estab-

lished by our Heavenly Father for sacred, holy and high purposes." (Ibid., p. 409.)

This, then, provides a sound basis for our teachings of sexual abstinence to contemporary young Latter-day Saints:

Sex is not something we avoid because it is evil.

Sex is something we wait for because it is good!

Chapter 6

SEVENTEEN STRATEGIES FOR TEACHING SEXUAL ABSTINENCE OUTSIDE MARRIAGE

Since it matters *how* we teach sexual morality, in this chapter I will share with you seventeen strategies that have worked for me. But first we should ask, *Who* should do the instructing or teaching?

For decades there has been a public discussion about who should teach young people about sexual matters. That debate has been fueled by the spread of AIDS. Who should teach the youth? The parents? School teachers? Religious leaders or instructors? Community or government leaders? Peers? The media? In actuality, all give information of one kind or another to young people—but often the information is either too bland to be helpful, too complex to be understood, given too late to be of any use, or contradictory with other information received.

The 1993 *Janus Report on Sexual Behavior* revealed some interesting insights on where young people today get their information about sexuality. In response to the question "I learned about sex from . . . ," 53 percent of the men stated "Streets/

Peers," 25 percent indicated "Home," 20 percent stated "School," and only 2 percent indicated "Church." Among women, 40 percent said they learned about it from "Home," 30 percent indicated "Streets/Peers," 28 percent listed "School," and, again, only 2 percent listed "Church." (Pp. 96–98.)

These numbers change for those who termed themselves "very religious." Among that group, 45 percent said their primary sources of sex information were either home or church. (Pp. 257–58.)

I think this study has tremendous implications for Latter-day Saints. It would be interesting to ask active young Latter-day Saints today what their primary source of sex information is. The results may be similar to the "very religious" youth just cited.

But what of the 60 or 70 percent who are not receiving their information from home or church? Peers, schools, community programs, and now the media are left to fill in the void.

As I indicated earlier, I am particularly concerned about the influence of the media on our youth. The numbers are frightening. How many suggestive commercials will a young person see at home, how many immoral television shows, how many provocative videos, how many suggestive magazines? How much questionable music will he or she hear? The influence of the media, and the media culture, is often greater than all other influences combined. As President Benson warned, "Too often television and movie screens shape our children's values." (*Teachings of Ezra Taft Benson,* p. 296.)

Ultimately, parents are in the best position to teach their children. The Church can help, sometimes appropriate community programs can help, but in the end the responsibility belongs to the parents. President Benson said:

> Parents should give their children specific instructions on chastity at an early age, both for their physical and moral protection. Years ago, President David O. McKay, God

bless him, read a statement written by Mrs. Wesley to her famous son John. I commend it to you as a basis for judgment pertaining to the matter of chastity. "Would you judge of the lawfulness or unlawfulness of pleasure? Take this rule: Now note, whatever weakens your reason, impairs the tenderness of your conscience, obscures your sense of God, takes off your relish for spiritual things, whatever increases the authority of body over the mind, that thing is sin to you, however innocent it may seem in itself." (Ibid., p. 278.)

A resource to LDS parents desiring educational materials for instructing young children on sexual matters is *A Parent's Guide*, published by The Church of Jesus Christ of Latter-day Saints in 1985. The manual contains units on teaching children about sexual matters from ages 1 to 3, 4 to 11, and 12 to 18. There is also a unit on teaching young adults about intimacy in marriage.

New Approaches Needed

If we Latter-day Saint parents are going to have any major impact on our children's understanding of sexual things, we will likely have to try some new approaches. In the past, we have often tried to *"make information safe for children."* We have tried to evaluate the television programs and movies our children watch. Some parents have gone to the public schools and critiqued in advance the sex-education programs that were to be presented to sons and daughters. We have wanted to know something about the teachers who would be presenting the material. We have been concerned about books available in public libraries. Some have confronted and boycotted businesses that sell questionable magazines and videos.

We should continue doing all these things, where appropriate and possible. But it is now evident to me that we, as parents or youth teachers or leaders, can no longer totally control what others (including the media) teach our young people about sexual relationships. It appears to be time for a new approach: *"We should make children safe for information."* That is, we should acknowledge the fact that at some place and some time our sons and daughters are going to see, read, or be taught something about sex and morality that is inconsistent with our own values. (It likely has already happened.) We must prepare them for such occasions by having ongoing discussions of what they have seen, read, or heard. We should continually teach and remind them of sexual values we wish to convey and also teach "correct principles" on sexual matters as made known through the scriptures and Church leaders.

Seventeen Strategies for Teaching Sexual Abstinence

While there have undoubtedly been many successful ways to teach sexual abstinence to Latter-day Saint youth, let me share with you some that have been particularly successful in my classes at BYU. Here are some of the strategies that have worked for me:

STRATEGY #1: Teach that sexual abstinence before marriage and sexual fidelity after marriage have been and are today commandments of the Lord. (See Exod. 20:12; Deut. 5:18; Matt. 19:18; Rom. 8:12; 13:9; Mosiah 13:22; Acts 15:20; 21:25; 1 Cor. 6:9; 6:13; 10:8; Gal. 5:19; 1 Thess. 4:3; D&C 42:24; 59:6; 66:10.) Like other commandments the Lord gives, he will prepare the way for us to live them if we make an effort to do so. (See 1 Ne. 3:7; 1 Cor. 10:13.)

STRATEGY #2: Teach of the great sexual sin the Lord foresaw, and revealed, concerning the latter days. Certainly those who want to align themselves with the Lord, rather than with Satan, will *not* want to be part of those trends. (See chapter 1.)

STRATEGY #3: Teach that modern prophets have warned that sexual impurity would be one of the great dangers that would threaten the Church from within in the last days. Those who are faithful will want to avoid being part of that threat. (See chapter 1.)

STRATEGY #4: Teach about the Second Sexual Revolution and the trends of sexual behavior among young people: (1) over 80 percent are sexually active by age 20; (2) sexually active young people now have a larger number of sexual partners; and (3) young people are becoming sexually active at a younger age. These are not trends that one would want to be part of. (See chapter 1.)

STRATEGY #5: Teach about the power the contemporary media can and often does have in shaping our attitudes, values, and even behavior in regard to sexual behavior. Do we want to be guided by the media or by the Lord and his prophets? (See chapter 2.)

STRATEGY #6: Teach about the rapid increase, even to epidemic proportions, not only of AIDS but of twenty to thirty other sexually transmitted diseases. Teach that some physicians suggest the only way these diseases will be controlled is through sexual abstinence or sexual restraint before marriage. (See chapter 3.)

STRATEGY #7: Teach (perhaps in private consultation or in small same-sex groups) the trends (and myths) regarding self-stimulation (masturbation). Indicate that even though it is common, there are many reasons why Latter-day Saints should not participate in this practice. (See chapter 4.)

STRATEGY #8: Teach that sexual abstinence before marriage does not limit freedoms but actually increases them.

Many young people are extremely sensitive about anyone—including parents, the government, teachers, or even Church leaders—suggesting rules or limitations of behavior. Having taken their cue from the "do your own thing" generation of the 1960s, many youth in the 1990s want to experiment and learn on their own and then decide what is best for them.

I saw this ideology firsthand while I was serving as a branch president at the Missionary Training Center in Provo. The recently called missionaries would arrive and kiss their loved ones good-bye; then the following night we would meet with them in their first branch meeting. By then they had received what came to be called the "White Bible," which had all the rules and guidelines for missionary conduct, not only while they were at the MTC but after they left for their various missions as well.

Upon receiving the White Bible some missionaries were upset. Why did they have to stay with their companions at all times? Why did they have to go to bed by 10:30 P.M. and get up at 6:00 A.M.? Why couldn't they wear sunglasses at the MTC, wear red suspenders (for the men), or multiple earrings (for the sisters)? (One sister at the MTC was particularly upset because she had just dyed her hair a strange color before arriving and had to have it re-dyed before she was allowed to continue on to her mission.) Why couldn't they call home whenever they wanted or have just a few guests while at the MTC? Why couldn't missionaries go down to the mall on their first "preparation day," and what was wrong with ordering a big pizza late at night for their district if they wanted one? Their complaints at times seemed endless. Some weren't ready for the rules or restrictions they were asked to follow.

Frankly, I got tired of trying to respond to their complaints while defending the White Bible. So I beat them to the punch and developed a little talk about "rules" which I gave the first night we met in branch meeting. I wrote on the board the following:

Rules are not given to limit our freedoms.
Rules are given to protect us from consequences.

I told them the White Bible was the culmination of many years of missionary experiences and they could learn from OPE (Other People's Experiences). They could learn the wisdom of the rules by trial and error—but if instead they would simply follow the rules and suggestions of those who supervised them, they would have a much more enjoyable mission.

Some young Latter-day Saints today likewise question the limitations and restrictions that are placed on their sexual behavior before marriage. We might appropriately say to them:

Commandments are not given to limit our freedoms.

Commandments are given to protect us from consequences.

In answer to the question "Why standards?" the First Presidency has noted:

> Standards are rules or guidelines given to help you measure your conduct. Why has the Lord given standards? He wants all his children to return to live with him one day. However, he knows that only those who are worthy will be able to live with him. Standards help you know how well you are preparing to live with your Father in Heaven. Your entire lives on earth are intended to give you the opportunity to learn to choose good over evil, service over selfishness, kindness and thoughtfulness over self-indulgence and personal gratification. By comparing your behavior and thoughts with your Father's standards, you are in a better position to govern yourselves and make the right choices. God's commandments (standards) are constant, unwavering, and dependable. As you adhere to them, you will receive countless blessings from heaven—including the gift of eternal life. (*For the Strength of Youth*, p. 6. Used by permission.)

STRATEGY #9: Teach that all our behaviors during our lives have consequences.

These consequences may be positive or negative, immediate or delayed. What's more, we seldom act in isolation, and the consequences of our behaviors almost always have an impact— good or bad, immediate or delayed—on the lives of other people.

Several years ago I was teaching at a large university where none of my students was a Latter-day Saint. One day in class a student asked me if I had ever committed adultery. I said no. He then asked why. It was a good question and at first I wanted to say that it violated one of the Ten Commandments and was a sin. But then I decided I wanted to give an answer that went beyond my religious values. So I wrote the following definition of maturity (which I made up on the spot) on the chalkboard:

MATURITY = *The ability to anticipate specific consequences of specific behaviors.*

I suggested that young children live for the day and have little interest in (or even knowledge of) "tomorrow" or the future. If you ask a young child to choose between having $1 today or $5 tomorrow, almost always he or she will choose the $1 for immediate use—there is no tomorrow. It is only as we get older that we understand some of the benefits of delayed gratification.

Like young children, the less mature young adult will often live for the moment. Because they are less mature, they are often unable to anticipate tomorrow's consequences of today's behaviors. People who gamble will go for the momentary thrill of winning and not understand they can lose a day's, month's, year's, or even a lifetime of earnings in just one brief evening. Cigarette smokers will enjoy the momentary high of nicotine in their systems, not accepting the fact that dangerous diseases, cancer, and even death can result in the future from the temporary pleasure of smoking. I explained to my students at the university that if I were to commit adultery, I would bring some serious consequences into my life, all of which I wanted to avoid. And I didn't have to experience adultery to know what the consequences would be. (I am a pretty good observer and learn from OPE—Other People's Experience.) I told my students that if I had sexual relationships outside of marriage I would likely have painful consequences in at least four areas of my life—physical, social, mental, and spiritual. If we are mature and observant, we can anticipate what some of these consequences will be *without* having to have the experience.

STRATEGY #10: Teach the *physical* consequences of sexual behavior outside of marriage.

First, to be honest and realistic, we must admit that there can and likely will be (1) some *momentary* pleasure and (2) some *momentary* peer acceptance from participation in such acts. The human body has the capacity to respond to sexual stimulus in a variety of ways because of the hedonistic ("it feels good") nature of sex. The media often depicts the pleasure associated with sexual relationships and passions, and I believe Satan uses such devices to try to draw us into illicit practices and behaviors. Many passionate moments are depicted in steamy bathroom scenes, bedrooms, or on the beach. *But the media seldom shows the resultant consequences of the sexual acts.*

The pleasure, as noted, is usually only momentary, often lasting just a few minutes. *In fact, there are few other acts of a shorter duration that have greater impact in our lives!* For just a few minutes (literally) of pleasure and thrill we can sometimes endure a lifetime of pain.

I told the students if I committed adultery I could father a child out of wedlock. Again, I didn't have to have the experience to anticipate the consequences. At that point, some people would contemplate abortion, which has its physical, social, mental, and spiritual ramifications as well.

Or I could become infected with a sexually transmitted disease, which could result in discomfort or even death.

Any or all of these painful consequences could have a lifelong effect. Is it worth it for a moment's pleasure?

STRATEGY #11: Teach the *social* consequences of sexual behavior outside of marriage.

Since we do not live in isolation, we will also likely experience social consequences of our behavior. Yes, there can be temporary social acceptance from indulging in sexual acts. But the desired attention soon fades if sexual pleasure was (as it often is) the only intended outcome of the experience.

Sexual acts outside of marriage are seldom, if ever, kept secret, at least not indefinitely. Someday the secret gets out, and those involved can experience varying degrees of social exclusion.

I told my students if I ever committed adultery, I would suffer social consequences in my relationships with my wife and children. I could anticipate in advance (with some maturity and insight) having to explain to Susan and our children what I had done. There could be a divorce, and the separation from both my wife and children would greatly affect all of us. If I weren't married, and became engaged, I might lose my fiancée if she wanted to marry a virgin and my past were ever discovered.

My students at this university were interested to know that I could be released from my Church calling if I committed adultery. I told them I was then serving as assistant to the minister in our congregation. (I was in the bishopric at the time.) They were amazed at that social consequence they had never imagined.

For Latter-day Saint youth there are many other social consequences that result from sexual experiences before marriage. A mission call may be delayed a year or more, depending on the frequency and nature of the sexual infraction. Or, if the sin is serious enough, there could be no mission call at all. Temple marriage can likewise be postponed for an indefinite period of time if

Latter-day Saints choose to engage in sexual relationships prior to marriage.

STRATEGY #12: Teach the *mental* consequences of sexual relationships outside of marriage.

I told my non-LDS students at the university if I committed adultery I would probably experience great guilt over the act. One student suggested that I paid too much attention to my conscience. An editor from a "men's" magazine had recently visited campus and encouraged the students to experiment with sexual behavior. He also advised them "not to feel guilty"—they had been reared, he claimed, in a sexually repressed society.

While it is true that too much guilt is damaging and detrimental, too little guilt is deadly to our spirits. Remember, the scriptures prophesy that in the last days "many will have their conscience seared with a hot iron" (1 Tim. 4:2), suggesting that they will become immune to the whisperings of their conscience.

Imagine yourself driving down the freeway and a light on your dashboard starts blinking. It has "water" written across the light, indicating your car is low on or out of water. You proceed a little farther and the light marked "oil" starts blinking, indicating your automobile also needs oil. You pay no attention to the blinking lights on your dashboard and just drive heedlessly on. Soon many lights are blinking—your car really needs attention. You can do one of two things: (1) stop the car and give it the service attention it needs, or (2) decide you don't like blinking lights on the dashboard, take a hammer, and knock them all out.

Your conscience could be compared to the lights on the dashboard. When it alerts you, something needs attention. You can choose to ignore it, or you can take the necessary actions and make the changes necessary.

The conscience can be a true guide in our lives. Mormon wrote: "It is given unto you to judge, that ye may know good from evil; and the way to judge is as plain, that ye may know with a perfect knowledge, as the daylight is from the dark night. For behold, the Spirit of Christ [which speaks through the conscience] is given to every man, that he may know good from evil." (Moro. 7:15–16.) Latter-day Saints also have the gift of the Holy Ghost or the Comforter, who "shall teach you all things, and bring all things to your remembrance." (John 14:26.)

Hopefully, Latter-day Saints will pay attention to these blinking "spiritual lights" as they appear in our lives. If we fail to do so, if we fail to forsake our sins and accept Jesus Christ and His atonement, we might pay the ultimate price in mental suffering and anguish. How severe will it be? The Lord revealed:

"Therefore I command you to repent—repent, lest I smite you by the rod of my mouth, and by my wrath, and by my anger, and your suffering be sore—how sore you know not, how exquisite you know not, yea, how hard to bear you know not.

"For behold, I, God, have suffered these things for all, that they might not suffer if they would repent;

"*But if they would not repent they must suffer even as I.*" (D&C 19:15–17; italics added.)

STRATEGY #13: Teach the *spiritual* consequences of sexual relationships outside of marriage.

With the increase of sexually transmitted diseases we should fear for our health, and even our very lives, when we engage in sexual relationships outside of marriage. As much as these deadly diseases are to be feared, however, physical death is not the greatest thing we should fear during mortality. The Lord has said, "Care not for the body, neither the life of the body; but care for the soul, and for the life of the soul." (D&C 101:37.) The destruction of the soul, or spirit, is of much greater consequence than the destruction of our physical bodies. And sexual behavior outside of marriage can greatly harm the health of our spirits. As we read in Proverbs 6:32, "Whoso committeth adultery with a woman lacketh understanding: he that doeth it destroyeth his own soul."

We sometimes wonder why a transgressor must wait a year or so before going to the temple or returning to the temple after committing acts such as fornication or adultery. Wouldn't the Lord want us to return as soon as possible?

The answer is no. By participating in unholy acts, we become unholy—and the Lord has revealed that "no unclean thing shall be permitted to come into [my] house to pollute it." (D&C 109:20; also see D&C 97:15–17.) When we commit serious sin, it usually takes time to become clean again.

It seems that sexual acts outside of marriage are so damaging to our spirits that they can't be healed quickly. If we beat our physical bodies with a baseball bat, they would be black and blue for several days or weeks, as they slowly recovered. Maybe such sexual acts have similar effects on our spirits, requiring a recovery time before we go (or return) to the temple, there to make covenants with the Lord to live righteous and pure lives.

STRATEGY #14: Teach that the pleasure from sex outside marriage is only temporary, while the pain often endures for some time.

Satan clearly seeks to induce youth, including Latter-day Saints, to engage in premarital sexual relations by placing great emphasis on the *pleasure* (however temporary) that comes with these experiences. Advertisements, magazines, videos, and movies portray such sexual experiences as something *very* desirable to do. Of course, those who put together such depictions are very good at what they do.

To counter the massive "sex-brings-pleasure" campaign that has been launched, Latter-day Saint parents and youth leaders can renew their own campaign that "fornication-brings-pain," emphasizing the *pain* that always follows inappropriate sexual experiences outside of marriage. If we hope to succeed, we have to "teach . . . diligently" (D&C 88:78) and be as skilled and effective in teaching as is our adversary.

STRATEGY #15: Teach the many personal benefits and blessings that come to those who wait until marriage for sexual relationships.

We previously noted that all behavior has consequences and outlined many of the painful physical, mental, social, and spiritual consequences that are experienced by those who do not sexually abstain until marriage. We should also teach the many positive consequences of waiting for marriage to have these intimate experiences. They include:

- Retaining your membership in Christ's restored church and enjoying the blessings that come with that membership, including partaking of the sacrament, paying tithing and fast offerings, and enjoying fellowship with the Saints.
- Having the constant companionship of the Holy Ghost in our lives.
- Experiencing no delay in a mission call or temple marriage.
- Having the confidence that comes from having virtuous thoughts. (See D&C 121:45–46.)
- Not having to worry about sexually transmitted diseases for yourself, your spouse (if he/she sexually abstained), and your children.
- Enjoying the strength of character and the spiritual development that comes from living God's commandments.
- Standing as candidates for entering the celestial kingdom after death if we continue to prove ourselves faithful.
- Having the happiness and peace of mind that come from observance of God's laws. (See Mosiah 2:41.)
- Being able to learn about sexual intimacy with only one person—your husband or wife, within the marital relationship.

One married student I taught at BYU, Chanalin Prina, wrote concerning the blessings of sexual morality:

Sex is a powerful thing. It has the power to unite two people in the most beautiful and complete way, while at the same time it has the power to destroy marriages and individuals completely. I think a lot of the problems young people have today in regard to sex are from improper examples and the lack of teaching the appropriateness of a sexual relationship. Somewhere in all the media the beauty of sex has been lost. It cannot be conveyed over a movie screen, in magazines, TV, or in pop rock. I think the beauty of sex can only be experienced in a proper marriage relationship where respect, love, and the Lord are the foundations. It should be taught in the home rather than in public places. And some parents are not taking the responsibility to teach their children appropriately. They leave those sacred teachings to others, where they are twisted and incorrectly perceived. . . .

The sexual desires we have are God-given and should always be regarded as such. Sex (when experienced appropriately in marriage) is not dirty, nor is it wrong. Unfortunately, some LDS youth grow up believing [otherwise]. I believe it is because we are always told what not to do, without much explanation why. Until recently, most of us have never been taught that sex is a beautiful union between husband and wife and that this [union] will only be enhanced by waiting until marriage.

I think it is important to focus on the benefits of waiting when teaching young people. If we can see how beautiful it can be, and how much more we will be able to cherish it, we will be more likely to wait, and less likely to be scared or have misconceptions about our future sexual relationships with our spouses.

Somehow we must help our youth understand that *the benefits of delayed sexual gratification until after marriage far outweigh the temporary pleasure of sexual indulgence while single!*

STRATEGY #16: Share the teachings of the latter-day prophets. Our apostles and prophets speak in behalf of the Lord, giving us guidance as they are inspired by God. Their words can be powerful aids as we seek to teach the youth of the Church.

President Ezra Taft Benson noted the predictable pain that will *always* follow sexual immorality. He said:

Some would justify their immorality with the argument that restrictions against it are merely religious rules, rules that are meaningless because in reality there is no God. This you will recognize is merely an untruthful rationalization designed to justify one's carnal appetite, lust, and passion. God's law is irrevocable. It applies to all, whether they believe in God or not.

Everyone is subject to its penalties, no matter how one tries to rationalize or ignore them. Immorality always brings with it attendant remorse. A person cannot indulge in promiscuous relations without suffering ill effects from it. He cannot do wrong and feel right—it is impossible.

Anytime one breaks a law of God, he pays a penalty in heartache, in sadness, in remorse, in lack of self-respect, and he removes himself from contact with the Spirit of God. Is it any wonder that those who indulge in sex relations outside of marriage deny God. (*Teachings of Ezra Taft Benson*, p. 281; italics added.)

President Benson also warned:

"If you fail as young people to properly restrain yourselves [sexually] you will pay the penalty in heartache, disappointment, and loss of self-respect. Do not reach out too eagerly for the excitements and thrills of life or they will turn to ashes in your hands. They will come in their own due time in the sacred bonds of marriage." (Ibid., p. 286.)

He similarly noted:

Do not be misled by Satan's lies. There is no lasting happiness in immorality. There is no joy to be found in breaking the law of chastity. *Just the opposite is true. There may be momentary pleasure. For a time it may seem like everything is wonderful.* But quickly the relationship will sour. Guilt and shame set in. We become fearful that our sins will be discovered. We must sneak and hide, lie and cheat. Love begins to die. Bitterness, jealousy, anger, and even hate begin to grow. *All of these are the natural results of sin and transgression.* (Ibid., p. 285; italics added.)

On the topic of the consequences of sexual sin, President Kimball noted:

There are many causes for human suffering—including war, disease, and poverty—and the suffering that proceeds from each of these is very real, but I would not be true to my trust if I did not say that *the most persistent cause of human suffering, that suffering which causes the deepest pain, is sin*—the violation of the commandments given to us by God. There cannot be, for instance, a rich and full life unless we practice total chastity before marriage and total fidelity after. There cannot be a sense of wholeness and integrity if we lie, steal, or cheat. There cannot be sweetness in our lives if we are filled with envy or covetousness. Our lives cannot really be abundant if we do not honor our parents. If any of us wish to have more precise prescriptions for ourselves in terms of what we can do to have more abundant lives, all we usually need to do is to consult our conscience. (*Teachings of Spencer W. Kimball,* p. 155; italics added.)

In 1990 the First Presidency gave the following admonitions to the young people of the Church:

You are not just ordinary young men and women. You are choice spirits who have been held in reserve to come forth in this day when the temptations, responsibilities, and opportunities are the very greatest. You are at a critical time in your lives. This is a time for you not only to live righteously but also to set an example for your peers. . . .

Your Father in Heaven is mindful of you. He has given you commandments to guide you, to discipline you. He has also given you your agency—freedom of choice—"to see if [you] will do all things whatsoever [He] shall command" (Abraham 3:25). Freedom of choice is a God-given, eternal principle that carries with it moral responsibilities for the choices made. We counsel you to choose to live a morally clean life. The prophet Alma declared, "Wickedness never was happiness" (Alma 41:10). Truer words were never spoken!

You cannot do wrong and feel right. It is impossible! Years of happiness can be lost in the foolish gratification of a momentary desire for pleasure. Satan would have you believe that happiness comes only as you surrender to his enticement to self-indulgence. We need only to look at the shattered lives of those who violate God's laws to know why Satan is called the "father of all lies" (2 Nephi 2:18). (*For the Strength of Youth,* pp. 3–5. Used by permission.)

STRATEGY #17: Finally, teach Doctrine and Covenants 100:16–17. It states:

"For I will raise up unto myself a pure people, that will serve me in righteousness;

"And all that call upon the name of the Lord, *and keep his commandments,* shall be saved."

Each time I give a lecture or talk at BYU on sexual behavior, I conclude by reading these verses. The Lord revealed that in the last days, prior to his second coming, people would generally be unrestrained when seeking sexual gratification. It appears we are now at that point. The Lord needs a people who will not join in such sexual sin, "a pure people," who will serve him in righteousness and help with his latter-day work with virtuous hearts and minds. (Also see D&C 43:14.)

Despite all our mortal imperfections, Latter-day Saints are that people! He is depending on us to help him build his kingdom. To be able to do so, we must keep ourselves pure and removed from worldly trends and wickedness. (For the importance of personal purity in the last days, see D&C 35:21; 38:8; 50:28–29; 56:18; 88:84; 97:16, 21; 112:28; 121:42; 124:54; and 136:11.)

In addition to these things, we must have the Holy Ghost in our lives, as we have discussed. To receive that great blessing, we must love God, "and purify [ourselves] before him." (D&C 76:116.)

The blessings of sexual abstinence before marriage are very great indeed. The consequences of sexual sin also are great. If we can help our youth to understand both blessings and consequences, we can go far toward teaching them to obey this most important commandment of the Lord.

Chapter 7

SPECIAL DIFFICULTIES
DURING ENGAGEMENT

We have already discussed how a high percentage (86 percent male, 80 percent female) of young single people in the United States have had sexual relationships by age nineteen. To turn those figures around, only 14 percent of men and 20 percent of women have sexually abstained up to that point in their life.

But that's only part of the story. The median age for marriage in the United States is currently about twenty-four for women and twenty-six for men. Since the above study deals only with the teen years, we need to realize that these nineteen year olds have, on average, another five to seven years before marriage. During these years, many men and women continue to have many opportunities to make choices about sexual abstinence.

It has been my observation while teaching at three major universities besides BYU that many young people have been taught to wait until marriage to engage in sexual relationships—and they fully intend to do so. Unfortunately, fewer and fewer actually make it to marriage without having had these experiences.

Among students who come from a religious background, many practice sexual abstinence during casual dating or the early part of the relationship. The difficulty comes when couples become serious, particularly if they decide to marry. After the official engagement, their desire to abstain sexually is challenged in new and powerful ways. There are, indeed, substantial difficulties during engagement.

Commitment Promotes Intimacy

There is a phenomenon noted in most college textbooks on marriage called the commitment/intimacy continuum. It is this: "The more committed we become in a relationship, the more likely it is that greater intimacy will occur." Let me explain.

When couples begin dating each other they have minimal commitment. They may go on one date and that's the end of it. Or, if they like each other, they may go on a second or third date. Perhaps they'll even continue dating until they are going steady and stop dating other people. Next, they may become engaged, with marriage following soon after. As their relationship develops, they go from minimum commitment (first date) to the maximum commitment of marriage.

The intimacy continuum progresses in the same way. They start with minimum intimacy, which usually begins with hand-holding. Next come arms on each other's shoulders or around the waist. Somewhere along the way, kisses, first of appreciation and then of affection, become part of the relationship.

Such exchanges of intimacy are appropriate. But some couples unwisely proceed to caressing or stroking various parts of the body (petting), which induces greater sexual pleasure, kissing parts of the body besides the mouth, touching each other below the waist, and finally sexual intercourse. On this continuum they start with minimum intimacy (hand-holding) and proceed to the maximum intimacy of full sexual relationships.

Some sociologists note that the two trends usually occur together. The more committed a couple become to each other, the more likely it is that greater intimacy will occur. In essence, commitment promotes intimacy.

Unaware of this trend, many engaged couples, including some Latter-day Saints, end up becoming more intimate with each other than they anticipated. Part of the reason is the "love makes it right" (or less wrong) ideology. I caution engaged students in my classes, telling them that if they want to wait until marriage for full intimacy they will have to be on guard, adjusting their behavior accordingly. During the engagement period many couples sometimes unknowingly overstimulate each other sexually. Frank discussions and appropriate adaptations should consequently follow.

A Needed Warning

I remember so well the day Susan and I became engaged. It was December 31, 1964. (We were married five months later, on June 5, 1965, in the Manti Temple.) For our engagement I took her to Temple Square and we stood between the Handcart and Seagull monuments, where I gave her an engagement ring. The next day we announced our engagement to our friends and classmates. It was a time of joy and excitement. The following Sunday, we went to church and announced our engagement to ward members and our bishop, T. Darrell Bushnell. He graciously congratulated us on our engagement and then invited us to a monthly meeting he held for all newly engaged couples in the ward. The meeting was held the following Sunday evening.

There were two or three other newly engaged couples who met with Susan and me and Bishop Bushnell. He again congratulated us on our engagements and then gave a rather stern warning about the sexual temptations that awaited us as we prepared for our wedding day. At first I was shocked at his firm warning.

Up to that point in our relationship we were physically attracted to each other but had been able to live the standards set by the Church. But once people become engaged to be married, values start doing crazy flip-flops as new temptations are faced.

Bishop Bushnell told us he had been the bishop of a BYU singles ward for some time. Many couples, he said, naively went into their engagements unaware of the new situation they were in. Temptations would increase, he said. The adversary would work overtime to prevent our temple marriages. We might find it easy to make excuses for behavior that earlier would have been out of the question.

He reviewed with us the questions we would later be asked in our temple recommend interviews. He also invited us to meet with him as often as needed to help us stay on track. He was, indeed, a wise bishop, and now, when I meet Bishop Bushnell in Provo where he still lives and works, I thank him for that frank talk and warning he gave Susan, me, and others that night in January 1965, just five months before our wedding.

Virtue Versus Purity

A few years later, after we were married and had started our family, Susan and I took the children to the movie *Pinocchio* one evening. In the movie, Jiminy Cricket and Pinocchio have a discussion on what is right and what is wrong. Jiminy Cricket says that "sin is something wrong that seems right at the time." I have used that quote often with engaged couples I've dealt with, trying to warn them of the temptations that await them. I have found that many LDS couples experience minimal temptations prior to their engagement. But after the engagement the temptations usually increase for all. Couples must take care that they don't do "something wrong" together, even if it "seems right at the time."

Sometime later I read a book by Elder Hugh B. Brown

called *You and Your Marriage*. Elder Brown made the point that most people can be virtuous if they are never tempted. But it is only after we resist temptation that we actually become pure. He observed:

"There is a distinction between innocence and purity. One is passive and the other active. Someone has paraphrased one of Ella Wheeler Wilcox's poems as follows:

It's easy enough to be virtuous
　　When nothing tempts you to stray,
When without and within no voice of sin
　　Is luring your soul away;
But it's only a negative virtue
　　Until it is tried by fire
And the soul that is worth the blessing of earth
　　Is the soul that resists desire.
(*You and Your Marriage*, p. 67.)

I suggest to single Latter-day Saints that they should never marry someone to whom they are not *physically* attracted. The vast majority of them are *sexually* attracted to their chosen mate. Because of this, I guarantee that almost all engaged couples will, as Elder Brown noted, be "tried by fire," the fire of desire. Hopefully, during this difficult time, they will also be among the souls that resist desire.

Love and Sex

While I was teaching at Southern Illinois University, one of the students in a class made an interesting observation. She said, "Men give love to get sex. And women give sex to get love." While that may or may not be the case after marriage, I can assure you that trend is in operation among many single people today. After much discussion in class, most of the two hundred students decided they agreed with her statement. Many single males do make statements of love as a means of enticing single women into a sexual relationship. And many single women engage in sexual relationships to seek to bring a single man into a love relationship.

One thing I learned from this experience is that, in the minds of many young women today, "love somehow makes it [sexual relationships] right." Or, if love doesn't make sex right, in some mysterious way it at least makes it "less wrong." I also learned from some of the single men in the class (most of whom admitted to experimentation with premarital sex) that they had specific ways or techniques of trying to convince young women they were "loved," hoping to increase the likelihood of sexual intimacy. Some claimed they could do so in just weeks or even, in a few cases, just days. I would hope that we wouldn't find such behavior among Latter-day Saints, but, unfortunately, I know of a few instances in which it has happened.

Genuine Love

The incidents just cited involved young couples who frequently had no intention of marriage. But what about the young couple who genuinely love each other and do intend to marry? They are also sometimes caught in the same philosophical shift and start believing that "love makes it right . . . or less wrong." This way of thinking appears to be a common trend among many young adults, including some Latter-day Saints.

Of course, such thinking is false and reflects a philosophy that Satan would have us embrace. I caution young couples that they need to resist such thoughts, to avoid all temptation to believe them, and certainly never to act on them.

Suggestions for Sexual Control during Engagement

When teaching at BYU about sexual abstinence before marriage, I give my students ten suggestions to help them avoid the added sexual temptations during the critical weeks or months of their engagement:

1. **REPENT OF PAST SINS.** If sexual sins have occurred in the past, either with the intended marriage partner or someone else, I encourage my students to immediately go to their LDS bishop and start the process of repentance so they can eventually marry in the temple. I read Doctrine and Covenants 58:43 to them, reminding them that proper repentance involves confessing and forsaking their sins. This includes past sexual sins, which will be forgiven only if they are confessed. (See D&C 61:2; 64:7.)

It is most important that those preparing to go to the temple not second-guess their bishops about their worthiness and the repentance process. Those who have committed a sexual transgression should get complete clearance from their bishop before sending out wedding invitations announcing marriage in the temple. No one should go to the temple unworthily—even if clearance takes a long time. The Lord has made it clear that he simply "will not be mocked" (D&C 63:58; 104:6; 124:71) by people lying or misrepresenting themselves in interviews with Church leaders.

2. **DECIDE NOW.** I suggest that when couples become engaged, they should verbally commit (or recommit) to sexual abstinence before marriage. They should also avoid the double standard of giving the young woman the primary responsibility for maintaining the standards. (In fact, many young women have told me their feeling that if the young man holds the priesthood, and particularly if he is a returned missionary, he holds the *greater* responsibility to see that sexual restraint is exercised.) Both male and female, I believe, mutually share the responsibility for sexual conduct before marriage. The agreement to abstain has to be open and clear, and it needs to be reviewed as often as necessary during the engagement.

3. AVOID LONG ENGAGEMENTS. My father, Alvin Barlow, served as a bishop and stake president for many years. He once told me he noticed that many couples who get involved in sexual transgressions also have long engagements. I have observed the same thing. Many young couples are unaware of the temptations that await them after they get engaged. They are equally unaware that familiarity creates familiarity—and that the longer they have to wait for sexual intimacy, the more difficult it is to do so.

How long is too long? I believe that once a couple decides to marry, they should marry as soon as possible. This implies that they have been careful in the first place in deciding to get married—the process of coming to a decision may take several months. But once the decision of *who* to marry is made, the *when* should generally follow quickly. Granted, it can take several months to plan a wedding. So an engagement of five or six months may be warranted. But beyond that, I believe young couples are setting themselves up for problems.

4. STAY OUT OF BEDROOMS. It is wise for engaged couples to stay out of bedrooms no matter how honorable the intentions may originally seem.

Bedrooms clearly have a sexual connotation; by avoiding them one can also lessen temptations.

Why would an engaged couple go into a bedroom? Some may innocently want to take a short nap on the bed, rather than lying on the front room floor or couch. Every year at BYU I have students tell me they often cannot get into their bedroom because roommates are in there "napping" with a boyfriend or girlfriend, planning a wedding, or doing any of a number of other things. Some of these activities may be appropriate in the living room, but it is my feeling that, for single people, *no* activity is appropriate in the bedroom. It's just too dangerous.

There is another caution I need to give. In recent years I've noticed an increase in what I call "sleep overs." A boyfriend will drive a long distance to date a young woman at BYU, and at the conclusion of the date he will end up sleeping in her front room. The excuse is that the weather is bad, it's too late to drive safely, and the young man has nowhere else to spend the night. Unfortunately, such situations are often just the beginning of future sexual interludes. Remember, Satan likes to lead us "carefully" to destruction. (2 Ne. 28:21.)

The first time or two the boyfriend will sleep on the couch, get up early the next morning, and leave. Next, he may sleep on the bed with his girlfriend, but both remain fully clothed. Nothing happens sexually for a time or two. Then, one evening all the other roommates are gone, and the couple retires to the bedroom. Only this time the clothing is removed, and you can guess the rest.

It is wise counsel to stay out of bedrooms for any reason. It is also wise to avoid these "sleep overs" at all costs. Surely the young woman knows of some other appropriate place where her date could spend the night.

5. LEARN TO CONTROL YOUR THOUGHTS. If it is true that "as we think so we become," then we should constantly guard our thoughts, particularly during the engagement period. Some engaged couples believe they can go to questionable PG-13 or even R-rated movies and come out unscathed. Or they believe they can watch provocative videos or read erotic magazines and not let it affect their behavior. They're wrong, of course. What we see affects what we think. And "as [a man] thinketh in his heart, so is he." (Prov. 23:7.)

It's true that sexual stimuli can come unsolicited to almost everyone in our sexually oriented society. But as one of my life-long friends, David Despain, has noted, "Just because a bird flies over your head, you don't have to let it build a nest in your hair." Modern revelation admonishes us to "let virtue garnish thy thoughts *unceasingly;* then shall thy confidence wax strong in the presence of God." (D&C 121:45; italics added.) Constantly allowing our thoughts to wander or dwell on sexual stimuli during the engagement period only increases the sexual pressure that many couples already feel.

6. RECOGNIZE THE LEVEL OF YOUR SEXUAL DEVELOPMENT. Some LDS couples who genuinely intend to wait until marriage for sexual relations end up not waiting for an unusual reason. Because they have so completely lived the law of chastity until that point in their lives, they are often quite naive. They either do not understand or else underestimate their level of sexual development.

Most couples can initially share appropriate types of affection such as holding hands and kissing and still stay well within the bounds of propriety. They often do not understand, however, that if they move to new levels of intimate behavior the circumstance becomes proportionally more difficult to control. Erotic kissing and caressing various parts of the body only lead to greater levels of intimacy. If such behavior occurs *frequently* and with great *intensity,* it is not a matter of *if,* but only a matter of *when* they will progress to sexual intercourse. Some engaged couples naively see how close to the edge of the cliff they can get without actually going over.

Other couples will become involved in what has become known as "technical virginity." They will not engage in sexual intercourse, hoping that they thereby can pass their temple recommend interview. But they *will* become involved in other types of inappropriate sexual behavior—including heavy petting with clothing removed or even oral sex—and yet believe they "technically" are virgins. The Church now gives local leaders the understanding that oral sex is a serious sin, and instructs those leaders to deal accordingly with single members engaging in such behavior.

Latter-day Saint students often ask in class, "Where do you draw the line when it comes to sexual intimacy before marriage?" I write on the board "Twelve Stages of Physical Intimacy" and then draw "The LDS Line":

Twelve Stages of Physical Intimacy

1. Eye to Body Contact
2. Eye to Eye Contact
3. Conversation (Talking to Each Other)
4. Holding Hands
5. Arms around Shoulders
6. Arms around Waist
7. Kissing or Face-to-Face Contact
8. Touching Face, Head, or Hair with Hand

The LDS Line

9. Touching/Stroking the Body (Petting)
10. Kissing Areas of Body Other Than Mouth
11. Touching below the Waist
12. Sexual Intercourse

(Adapted from Desmond Morris, *Intimate Behavior* [New York: Random House, 1971], pp. 71–78.)

Stages 1 to 8 are entirely appropriate for LDS engaged couples, but care should be taken in proceeding past the line. Those who do cross that line are putting themselves at great risk—and if they do so *frequently* and *intensely* they will almost certainly progress to the point of sexual intercourse.

7. MEET WITH BISHOP(S) OFTEN. The Lord wants all members of the Church to attend the temple. He just doesn't want us to do so unworthily because of the higher laws and more disciplined life we there covenant to live.

I suggest in my marriage classes that bishops should be seen as allies and not enemies when it comes to temple worthiness.

When a Church member desires to enter the temple, he or she must receive the endorsement of two elders of Israel (usually the bishop and stake president), signifying his or her worthiness to enter. I encourage newly engaged couples to meet with their bishop soon after their engagement. Ask him to review the temple recommend questions. Also ask him to help define the appropriate boundaries for affection during the engagement period.

If a couple feels unduly tempted, fearing they are "approaching the edge of the cliff," they should meet with their bishop as soon as possible; doing so may help them to avoid transgression. Bishops and stake presidents are experienced in dealing with such situations and couples should take advantage of their expertise and spiritual help for precautionary purposes.

8. CHOOSE PEERS WISELY. During the engagement period, LDS engaged couples should choose carefully the individuals or couples with whom they associate. Peer influence can be great in all areas, including sexual behavior, so associates should be chosen who share the same values. Even engaged couples with good intentions can eventually yield to sexual temptations if they continually associate with other couples, married or single, who engage in inappropriate sexual conduct. As Paul admonished, "from such turn away." (2 Tim. 3:5.)

9. AVOID FATIGUE AND ISOLATION. Some engaged LDS couples valiantly combat sexual temptations during this critical period only to yield once they become either fatigued or isolated. I believe there is a direct correlation between physical fatigue and a lessened ability to resist sexual stimuli. In other words, the more tired we are, the less likely it is we'll resist temptation. Since this is the case, engaged couples should avoid activities such as skiing for many hours, long hikes, or overnight camping trips (a bad idea anyway) where great physical energy is exerted. They should also avoid late dates—I suspect most sexual transgression occurs after midnight.

10. USE DISCRETION WITH PRAYER. In latter-day revelation we are encouraged to pray to conquer Satan (D&C 10:5), to resist temptation (D&C 20:33), and to restrict Satan's power over us (D&C 93:49). Because of this, it would seem practical for an engaged couple to pray individually and as a couple—these blessings are much needed by us all. But it would be wise to pray together only during the day and to use discretion in "couple prayers."

When Susan and I became engaged while attending BYU, a General Authority gave a devotional address that discouraged engaged couples from praying together in intimate settings. He particularly suggested that engaged couples not go into bedrooms to pray. Furthermore, he noted that prayer can help create added intimacy between a man and a woman and is encouraged with married couples for that reason. But engaged couples should pray together only with caution.

I believe it may be appropriate for a couple to pray together at the beginning of a date or the beginning of a long trip. But extended prayers in isolation, particularly late at night, should be avoided by LDS engaged couples striving for sexual abstinence prior to marriage.

Prepare and Prevent

During our struggles to live the law of chastity during the engagement period we should keep in mind that (1) temptations and problems are common to all; (2) Heavenly Father will never allow us to be tempted beyond our capacity to withstand temptation; and (3) he will help provide means whereby we can overcome our temptations in life.

Paul wrote: "There hath no temptation taken you but such as is common to man: but God is faithful, who will not suffer you to be tempted above that ye are able; but will with the temptation also make a way to escape, that you may be able to bear it." (1 Cor. 10:13; see also 1 Ne. 3:7.)

President Ezra Taft Benson gave some valuable counsel on chastity that has specific relevance for engaged couples who are preparing for a temple marriage. He said, "When it comes to the law of chastity, it is better to prepare and prevent than it is to repair and repent."

He then gave a few suggestions to help single people avoid sexual transgression. Engaged couples who follow them will surely reach their goal of a worthy temple marriage. President Benson said: "Decide now to be chaste. Control your thoughts. Always pray for the power to resist temptation. . . . For those who are single and dating members of the opposite sex, carefully plan positive and constructive activities so that you are not left to yourselves with nothing to do but share physical affection." (*Teachings of Ezra Taft Benson*, pp. 284–85.)

Chapter 8

FOR THOSE
WHO HAVE SINNED

All who become disciples of Jesus Christ have to reconcile their past sinful behavior with their present desire to become righteous, "for all have sinned and come short of the glory of God." (Rom. 3:23.)

All have sinned, but there is hope. John taught: "If we say that we have no sin, we deceive ourselves, and the truth is not in us. If we confess our sins, he [Christ] is faithful and just to forgive us our sins, and to cleanse us from all unrighteousness." (1 John 1:8–9.)

When we get discouraged because of our sins, we must remember that the Lord is eager for us to repent and be forgiven. Even many of his valiant disciples had to repent of a sinful past before they could move ahead as servants of the Lord. Let me give you some examples.

Most are aware of the conversion of Alma the younger and the four sons of Mosiah, who, before their repentance, "were the very vilest of sinners" (Mosiah 28:4) and even sought to destroy the church (Mosiah 27:10; Alma 26:18). Alma the elder also had an unrighteous past prior to his conversion. He wrote:

"Remember the iniquity of king Noah and his priests; and I myself was caught in a snare, and did many things which were abominable in the sight of the Lord, which caused me sore repentance;

"Nevertheless, after much tribulation, the Lord did hear my cries, and did answer my prayers, and has made me an instrument in his hands in bringing so many of you to a knowledge of his truth." (Mosiah 23:9–10.)

Even mighty Nephi lamented his sins. He wrote:

"Notwithstanding the great goodness of the Lord, in showing me his great and marvelous works, my heart exclaimeth: O wretched man that I am! Yea, my heart sorroweth because of my flesh; my soul grieveth because of mine iniquities.

"I am encompassed about, because of the temptations and the sins which do so easily beset me.

"And when I desire to rejoice, my heart groaneth because of my sins; nevertheless, I know in whom I have trusted." (2 Ne. 4:17–19.)

The Apostle Paul was deeply concerned about the sins he'd committed before he was converted to Jesus Christ. He had witnessed and consented to the stoning and death of Stephen and "made havock of the church, entering into every house, and haling men and women committed them to prison." (Acts 8:1–3; also see Acts 7:54–60.) On several occasions he was active in the persecution of the Saints and did many things "contrary to the name of Jesus of Nazareth." (Acts 26:9–10; also see Gal. 1:13.) After acknowledging his past persecutions of the church (Philip. 3:6), he did the only thing one can do who has sinned and desires to serve the Lord:

"This one thing I do, *forgetting those things which are behind,* and reaching forth unto those things which are before, I press toward the mark for the prize of the high calling of God in Christ Jesus." (Philip. 3:13–14; italics added.)

In modern times we have similar examples of those who were anxious to be forgiven of past sins. Though the youthful sins of young Joseph Smith are not identified, he wrote of his youth:

"I was left to all kinds of temptations; and, mingling with all kinds of society, I frequently fell into many foolish errors, and displayed the weakness of youth, and the foibles of human nature; which, I am sorry to say, led me into divers temptations, offensive in the sight of God. In making this confession, no one need suppose me guilty of any great or malignant sins. A disposition to commit such was never in my nature. But I was guilty of levity, and sometimes associated with jovial company not consistent with that character which ought to be maintained by one who was called of God as I had been." (JS-Hist. 1:28.)

Of the night when the angel Moroni first appeared to Joseph Smith, Joseph wrote: "I often felt condemned for my weakness and imperfections; when on the evening of the above-mentioned twenty-first of September, after I had retired to my bed for the night, I betook myself to prayer and supplication to Almighty God for forgiveness of all my sins and follies, and also for a manifestation to me, that I might know of my state and standing before him." (JS-Hist. 1:29.)

As others joined the Church after the restoration, they likely had similar concerns about past sins. The Lord frequently revealed that if they would go forth to preach the gospel they would bring salvation to their own souls (see D&C 4:4; 11:3; 12:3; 14:3) and would be forgiven of their previous sins (see D&C 31:5; 62:3; 84:61).

If Sexual Transgressions Have Occurred

The ideal pattern would be for all young members of the Church to follow the Lord's admonition to wait until marriage for sexual relationships. Many do. Some don't. And if Latter-day Saints follow current trends, an increasing number will fall into the category of those who have not waited. What might be done or said to those who have sinned? Is all hope lost for forgiveness? Can they repent? Can they become virtuous again? Can they even go forth and teach the laws of chastity to others when they, themselves, were not able at first to abide by the teachings of the Lord?

The answer lies in the story of Corianton. Corianton committed the great sin of going in to the harlot, Isabel—and he did so while he was on his mission! His father, Alma the younger, confronted him, saying, "Thou didst do that which was grievous unto me; for thou didst forsake the ministry, and did go over into the land of Siron among the borders of the Lamanites, after the harlot Isabel. Yea, and she did steal away the hearts of many, but this was no excuse for thee, my son. Thou shouldst have tended to the ministry wherewith thou wast entrusted." (Alma 39:3–5.)

The sinful behavior of Corianton hindered the missionary endeavors of his father, who further counseled: "Suffer not yourself to be led away by any vain or foolish thing; suffer not the devil to lead away your heart again after those wicked harlots. Behold, O my son, how great iniquity ye brought upon the Zoramites; for when they saw your conduct they would not believe in my words." (Alma 39:11.)

Often our understanding of Corianton's life stops there. But we should read on. Alma counseled Corianton to "turn to the Lord with all your mind, might, and strength" and return to the Zoramites and "acknowledge your faults and that wrong which ye have done." (Alma 39:13.) Then, after teaching Corianton pertinent gospel concepts (Alma 40–42), Alma told his son to go forth on his mission: "And now, O my son, ye are called of God to preach the word unto this people. And now, my son, go thy way, declare the word with truth and soberness, that thou mayest bring souls unto repentance, that the great plan of mercy may have claim upon them." (Alma 42:31.)

Apparently Corianton followed the counsel of his father, repented of his sins, went on his mission, and remained faithful to the Lord's teachings. At the end of the book of Alma we read: "And [Shiblon] was a just man, and he did walk uprightly before God; and he did observe to do good continually, to keep the commandments of the Lord his God; and also did his brother." (Alma 63:2.) Since Shiblon's older brother, Helaman, had already died (Alma 62:52), it seems likely that the righteous brother described in this verse is Corianton (also see Alma 49:30; 63:10).

The Past, Present, and Future

While I was serving as a branch president at the Missionary Training Center in Provo, Utah, I interviewed an elder who doubted his ability to be a worthy missionary. He said he had committed many sexual sins in his life, all of which he had confessed to his bishop and stake president. Some of his sins were serious enough that his mission call was delayed while he further confessed to a General Authority of the Church. Finally, he was cleared for missionary service.

Even though he had confessed and forsaken his sins (see D&C 58:43), he was still worried about his ability to be an effective missionary. I suggested he become a modern Corianton. At first he was shocked at the suggestion. Like many others, he was familiar only with Corianton's escapade with Isabel, not with his subsequent repentance and service. We read together Alma's call for Corianton to return to the Lord with all his "mind, might and strength" and to go forth preaching the gospel. We read the other scriptures that indicated Corianton's response as he became a faithful missionary and disciple.

During the course of our lengthy discussion that night I

suggested that *the present is more important than the past.* All we can do about our past is turn from it, repent, and learn from it. (See D&C 67:14.) I also stated my belief that, in some ways, *the future is more important than the present.* All of us can "become," and choose to travel in new, more worthy paths than we have taken in the past.

The elder left that night still not certain he could overcome a riotous past and serve a faithful mission. Later, when he arrived in the mission field, he wrote me a letter and thanked me for our discussion while he was in the Missionary Training Center. He said he was trying to become a modern Corianton and thanked me for the thought written at the bottom of his letter:

"What we are is more important than what we have been;

And what we can become is more important than what we are."

I believe this insight is still significant for many other "Coriantons" who have sinned, have genuinely repented by confessing and forsaking their sins, and now have a true desire to serve the Lord.

Once Lost, Can Virtue Be Regained?

Young Latter-day Saints who have had sexual experiences prior to marriage may wonder if they can become virtuous again. If they repent can virtue be regained completely or just partially? It is a good question that deserves some attention.

When I was a young boy growing up in the Church I once had a sobering lesson on chastity. For a visual aid, the teacher brought to class a board, a nail, and a hammer. During his lesson he hammered the nail into the board and said, "That is sin." Then he pulled the nail out of the board and said, "That is repentance." Finally, he drew our attention to the hole that remained in the board and said that even though we repented there would always be a hole in the board. We could not, he suggested, totally regain our virtue.

That was a powerful lesson to a group of young Latter-day Saints in their early teens. I left his lesson that day fully believing that once you had "lost your virtue" you could never totally regain it.

A few years later we had a similar lesson from another teacher. She, too, brought the board, hammer, and nail, but she also brought a can of wood putty. She hammered the nail in the board, pulled it out, and then gave a magnificent lesson on the atonement of Christ. She put the wood putty in the hole to symbolize that once we sin, we can, through proper repentance, become totally virtuous again. She concluded her lesson with a quotation from Isaiah: "Come now, and let us reason together, saith the Lord: though your sins be as scarlet, they shall be as white as snow; though they be red like crimson, they shall be as wool." (Isa. 1:18.) I've always been grateful for that can of wood putty our teacher brought to class. But now I understand that when we truly repent, the power of the atonement is so great it doesn't just cover over our sins—it's as though the Savior gives us a new board!

Our prophets have clearly taught about the power of Christ to cleanse us. President Ezra Taft Benson said:

There may be some for whom the counsel to prepare and prevent is too late. You may already be deeply entangled in serious sin. If this is the case, there is no choice now but to repair your lives and repent of your sins. *To you I would suggest five important things you can do to come back to a state of moral purity:* (1) Flee immediately from any situation you are in that is either causing you to sin or that may cause you to sin; (2) Plead with the Lord for the power to overcome; (3) Let your priesthood leaders help you resolve the transgression and come back into full fellowship with the Lord; (4) Drink from the divine fountain and fill your lives with positive sources of power; and (5) Remember that through proper repentance, *you can become clean again.* For those who pay the price required by true repentance the promise is sure. *You can be clean again.* The despair can be lifted. The sweet peace of forgiveness will flow into your lives. In this dispensation the Lord spoke with clarity when he said: "Behold, he who has repented of his sins, the same is forgiven, and I, the Lord, remember them no more" (D&C 58:42). (*Teachings of Ezra Taft Benson,* p. 284; italics added.)

Second Virginity

During the past few years a term has been coined to describe an admirable trend. It is called "Second Virginity." Some young people who have had sexual experiences, and then experience the remorse and other consequences that follow, suddenly realize that sexual abstinence is best after all. They then choose to enter into what is called a "Second Virginity," where they practice and advocate sexual abstinence prior to marriage.

Of course, for Latter-day Saints it is not enough simply to change behavior. Forgiveness and cleansing come only when we truly repent.

Young people who choose to enter their Second Virginity should be careful, because once a person has become involved in sex it is much easier to become involved the second time. I have noticed in my counseling of many young people that the temptation is much greater (perhaps seven times!) the "second time around" because of patterns of behavior that have now been learned. (See Matt. 12:43–45.) Greater care, caution, and concern must be exhibited by one who desires to remain abstinent after having been involved in inappropriate sexual behavior.

In some ways the Second Virginity philosophy is commendable and is undoubtedly experienced by some Latter-day Saints. There is a danger, however, for young Latter-day Saints to believe they can sin sexually and then merely enter the Second Virginity stage with little or no consequences.

I recently became aware of a young Latter-day Saint couple who seemed to emphasize the letter rather than the spirit of the law of chastity. They drove to another state where they were married in a civil ceremony. Following the ceremony they spent a three-day honeymoon in a local motel. Then they went through the appropriate legal channels, had their marriage annulled, and returned home.

Had sin been committed? They were "legally" married during the days they engaged in sexual intimacy. But was their conduct inappropriate? Their weekend escapade became known to their bishop. What should he have done?

Should he have held a disciplinary council? If the naive young couple later desired to be married to others in the temple, should recommends be granted? Should any repentance or period of probation be required before going to the temple?

When We Sin Knowingly

People who sin unknowingly or ignorantly will not be judged as harshly as those who have been taught otherwise. Alma noted that "good and evil have come before all men; he that knoweth not good from evil is blameless." (Alma 29:5.)

But those who sin knowingly (as did the young couple in the above example) will have to answer for their actions. Nephi, who witnessed the fall of the Nephites prior to the visitation of the Savior, wrote of them: "Now they did not sin ignorantly, for they knew the will of God concerning them, for it had been taught unto them; therefore they did willfully rebel against God." (3 Ne. 6:18; also see 4 Ne. 1:38; Morm. 1:16.) James likewise noted: "To him that knoweth to do good, and doeth it not, to him it is sin." (James 4:17. Used by permission.)

In 1990 the LDS First Presidency expressed similar concerns:

> Some people knowingly break God's commandments. They plan to repent before they go on a mission or receive the sacred covenants and ordinances of the temple. Repentance for such behavior is difficult and painful and may take a long time. It is better to not commit the sin. Certain sins are of such gravity that they can put your membership in the Church and your eternal life at risk. Sexual sins are among those of such seriousness. (*For the Strength of Youth,* p. 17. Used by permission.)

But if we have sinned, we must not think all is lost. The First Presidency reminds us of the blessing of repentance:

> Where choices have already led to sexual impurity, repentance is the way back. Talk to your parents and your bishop. They love you and will explain to you how to repent and put your life in order again. Follow their counsel.
>
> The miracle of forgiveness is real, and true repentance is accepted by the Lord. Full repentance of some sins requires that we not only confess and resolve them with the Lord but that we also do so with the Church. The bishop and stake president have been appointed by revelation to serve as judges in these cases.
>
> Only the Lord can forgive sins, but these priesthood leaders can assist the transgressor in the process of repentance. In serious cases of transgression, Church disciplinary action could be required and disfellowshipment or

excommunication could result. These actions are taken only when they are necessary in the repentance process. If you have sinned, the sooner you begin to make your way back, the sooner you will find the sweet peace and joy that come with the miracle of forgiveness.

As you follow these guidelines, you will feel and experience the power of the Spirit of the Lord, you will come to know the truth, and you will gain confidence in yourself and the Lord. The Savior taught, "The truth shall make you free" (John 8:32). As you grow in that truth and freedom, you will experience the peace of the Lord Jesus Christ, a peace that brings great strength. (*For the Strength of Youth,* pp. 17–18. Used by permission.)

Satan Dwells on Our Past

It has been my observation that once we have repented, Satan wants us to continue to pay a great amount of attention to our sinful pasts. He does this, I believe, to prevent us from concentrating on current opportunities to mature and grow, and to love and serve others. Remember, Satan is a miserable person who wants to make others miserable like unto himself. (See 2 Ne. 2:27.)

Not long ago I had a conversation with a woman who was serving as Young Women's president in her stake. She was a beautiful woman and was doing a wonderful job in her calling. But she confided that she was sometimes uncomfortable in her service because of sexual sins she had committed as a young woman growing up in the Church. These sexual experiences constantly returned to her mind as she was serving in her current Church calling, and she couldn't get rid of them. She asked me for advice.

I suggested to her that we often get into the saint/sinner

mentality in the Church, thinking that others are either all saint or all sinner. Of course, we all are a mixture of both. And what of the sinner in us? I recalled a quotation I had learned on my mission, penned by the Scottish poet Robert Burns. He observed that "Saints are just sinners who keep on trying."

Anyone who goes into a helping profession—whether it be in a career, as a church leader, or as a community worker—has to deal with the reality of his or her own imperfections. I told the woman that when I got into marriage counseling I occasionally felt I couldn't help others because of my own imperfections. But one of my teachers at Florida State University (a former Methodist minister) gave me both comfort and encouragement. He emphasized again and again: "One imperfect person can help another imperfect person."

The Young Women's president was encouraged as I had been. Even though we are all imperfect human beings, we can learn to "bear one another's burdens, [and] comfort those that stand in need of comfort." (Mosiah 18:8–10.) As parents, teachers, and even leaders, our weak traits or characteristics can become our strengths—if we will learn to come unto Christ, be humble, have faith, and receive his grace. (See Eth. 12:27.)

Go in Peace

Finally, I suggested that this Young Women's president go home and reread Luke 7:36–50. To me, this is one of the most inspiring and sensitive accounts in scripture. It is almost like a short one-act play with three people: A Pharisee named Simon, a woman identified as a "sinner," and Jesus. Simon had invited Jesus to come to his home and eat with him. After Jesus sat down, the woman, "a sinner," began to anoint his feet with ointment. As she did so she wept, washing his feet with her tears, then wiping them with the long hair of her head. Simon was offended, and said "within himself" that Jesus obviously wasn't really a prophet—if he were, he would know the woman was a sinner and would not allow her to touch him.

Jesus apparently perceived Simon's thoughts, and gave unto him a parable:

"There was a certain creditor which had two debtors; the one owed five hundred pence, and the other fifty. And when they had nothing to pay, he frankly forgave them both. Tell me therefore, which of them will love him the most?" (Vv. 41–42.)

Simon thought it over and said "I suppose that he, to whom he forgave most." Jesus answered, "Thou hast rightly judged." (V. 43.)

Then, while Simon seemed to want to dwell on the woman's sinful past, Jesus shifted focus, pointing out her present commendable acts. He noted that she had washed his feet and kissed them, and had anointed them with oil. Simon, on the other hand, had failed to give Jesus water for his feet, had given him no kiss of greeting, and had not honored Jesus by anointing his head with oil.

Jesus then said: "Her sins, *which are many*, are forgiven; for she loved much; but to whom little is forgiven, the same loveth little. And he said unto her, Thy sins are forgiven." (Vv. 47–48; italics added.)

His final words to the woman were, "Thy faith hath saved thee; *go in peace*." (V. 50; italics added.)

There is a magnificent lesson in this biblical episode, particularly since, as we noted in the beginning of this chapter, "all have sinned." We, too, must become like the woman in Simon's house, put our sins behind us through proper repentance, and then "go in peace" and no longer be troubled by our sinful past.

Perhaps some young Latter-day Saint men and women have not yet accepted a mission call because they have sinned and have not yet confessed, repented, and forsaken the sin. They should do so now—and then "go in peace."

Maybe others are putting off a temple marriage because of a sinful past. They should repent by confessing and forsaking their sins, meet all the requirements given by their bishop and stake president, and then do as Paul did: "[Forget] those things which are behind." (Philip. 3:13.) Having gone through the process of repentance, they should go worthily to the temple—and they should "go in peace."

Maybe there are those who are being taught the gospel by the missionaries and are hesitant to proceed because of a sinful past. Some may feel unworthy to be baptized and then serve in a Church calling. Male converts may feel uncertain about receiving the priesthood because of sins they have committed. Such potential members should likewise properly repent by confessing and forsaking their sins, and then go forth to be baptized, symbolically washing away their sins and enabling them to start anew. (D&C 20:37.) Then, after being baptized and receiving the gift of the Holy Ghost, these new members should remember that the Lord forgets their sins—and so should they. (See Isa. 1:18; D&C 58:42–43.) With these blessings, they can move forward in newness of life—and as they progress, they should "go in peace."

So with all of us. The Lord abhors sin, but he forgives those who are truly penitent. And then, even though our past sins may be "as scarlet," we can "go in peace," for the Lord, in his love, will make them "white as snow."

Chapter 9

COMMON QUESTIONS
AND ANSWERS

After we have discussed strategies for sexual abstinence before marriage, I typically give my students at BYU the opportunity to ask questions about sexual matters. Here are some of the questions they most frequently ask:

1. Is sex so sacred that it needs to be secret?

Sexual relationships in marriage are indeed sacred, and traditionally they have been kept secret as well. We have been clear about the "shalt nots" of sex, but have not said so much about the "shalts." But there is so much information on sexuality now available in the world that it seems wise for us to go on the offensive, to present a gospel view of healthy sexuality. "Ignorance is not bliss," and "What you don't know, *can* hurt you." Remember the statement by President Kimball that sexual incompatibility is, in his opinion, the main cause of divorce among Latter-day Saints. (See Chapter 5 for further discussion on the importance of having adequate information about sex both before and after marriage. Also see Brent A. Barlow, "They Twain Shall Be One," *Ensign*, Sept. 1986, p. 49.)

---

2. If you practice sexual abstinence before marriage, how do you know you will be sexually compatible afterward?

This is an excellent question and one that frequently arises in my classes at BYU. I believe there are at least three elements in a relationship before marriage that can indicate the degree of sexual compatibility afterward: (1) The couple should be comfortable touching each other (holding hands, arms around each other, embracing, and so forth) during the dating and engagement period; (2) The couple should feel comfortable sharing appropriate kisses of affection before marriage; and (3) The couple should anticipate and genuinely look forward to becoming more sexually intimate with each other once they are married. When any of these conditions are not met prior to marriage, I seriously question whether the couple is ready to marry, speaking in terms of sexual compatibility.

3. How do I know if what I'm feeling for my fiancé is love or lust?

Whenever I teach classes that have a large number of engaged couples, the question of love versus lust always arises. To be honest, most of us have some experience with lust as we are growing up. It is an intense sexual passion or attraction to some person or object (including picture or video), with little or no sentiments of love. It is a fantasy or desire for sex simply for sex's sake.

In the vast majority of cases at BYU, young couples do love each other and experience genuine feelings of attraction and admiration. But because sexual feelings are also involved, engaged couples ask time and time again, "What is it we are feeling? Is it love or is it lust?"

My answer is that it could be either, or a combination of both.

I have had some interesting discussions with other professional people about whether or not it is possible for a married husband and wife to "lust" after each other. If lust is defined as an intense sexual passion or attraction to some person or thing, with little or no sentiments of love, then yes, lust can occur in marriage. But I would like to think that much of the physical attraction that married people have for each other is based on the element of love.

The same must be said of most engaged couples. I believe that most relationships are based on genuine love—but couples still need to exercise restraint and control to keep themselves morally pure until the marriage has occurred.

4. Are feelings of lust the same as adultery?

A scripture that sometimes causes concern for many young people is found in Matthew 5:28: "Whosoever looketh on a woman [or man] to lust after her [or him] hath committed adultery . . . already in his [her] heart." If a young person is physically attracted to another person or even "lusts" after them, is he or she the same as the adulterer or one who acts out the thought? Or suppose a young boy or girl has fantasized during self-stimulation, as apparently many have. Is he or she then in the same category as fornicators or adulterers?

President Joseph F. Smith once noted there are differing degrees of sexual sins. He observed:

> There are said to be more shades of green than of any other color, so also we are of the opinion there are more grades or degrees of sin associated with the improper relationship of the sexes than of any other wrongdoing of which we have knowledge. They all involve a grave offense—the sin against chastity, but in numerous instances this sin is intensified by the breaking of sacred covenants, to which is sometimes added deceit, intimidation or actual violence.

> Much as all these sins are to be denounced and

deplored, we can ourselves see a difference both in intent and consequence between the offense of a young couple who, being betrothed, in an unguarded moment, without premeditation fall into sin, and that of the man who having entered into holy places and made sacred covenants, plots to rob the wife of his neighbor of her virtue either by cunning or force to accomplish his vile intent." (*Gospel Doctrine*, pp. 388–89.)

If, as with the reasoning of President Joseph F. Smith, adultery is more serious than fornication, and adultery committed by those who have been through the temple far more serious than those who have not been there, then it seems that thoughts or feelings of lust, though sinful, are not as serious as the acts.

5. What do you need to know or discuss about sex with your fiancé before marriage?

There are several key areas regarding sexuality that require discussion by an engaged couple prior to marriage:

a. Ask if you are physically attracted to each other, as discussed in question #2 above.

b. Have a long, serious discussion about children, including how many are desired, when to start having them, and how close together they should be born.

c. If you decide that you do not want to have a child immediately (e.g., a honeymoon pregnancy), you will have to make appropriate plans before the wedding.

d. If you don't want your honeymoon to overlap with the onset of the new wife's menstruation, you'll need to plan accordingly.

e. If either of you have questions that require medical skills or advice, schedule premarital exams with a competent physician. Many couples desire to see an active LDS physician so questions asked during the exam might be answered within the gospel framework. Many couples arrange for a premarital exam at the same time as a blood test if they are to be married in a state that requires one.

6. Should I discuss past sexual sins with my fiancé?

As one prepares for marriage, there is a natural inclination to want to know whether or not your partner has been sexually involved with others. I typically advise young people *not* to share their sexual pasts with each other. Most young people are not mature enough to handle that kind of information early in the relationship. And unfortunately, the confessed sexual past can later be used as a weapon in arguments on other subjects. Certainly all sexual transgressions should be confessed to priesthood leaders, but I believe that couples should be obligated to share such information with each other only if the transgression took place after they started dating each other.

If either party insists on knowing about sexual pasts, it is better to discuss them long before the marriage date, rather than waiting.

The possibility of being required to reveal your sexual past is, all by itself, a major reason to practice sexual abstinence before marriage. I have known some instances where the marriage was canceled after such information was exchanged.

I do need to give a warning, though. If the errant party has confessed and forsaken the sin, and has been forgiven by both the Church and the Lord, there is great danger in judging him or her harshly. Latter-day revelation declares: "Wherefore, I say unto you, that ye ought to forgive one another; for he that forgiveth not his brother his trespasses standeth condemned before the Lord: for there remaineth in him the greater sin. I, the Lord, will forgive whom I will forgive, but of you it is required to forgive all men." (D&C 64:9–10.)

This commandment applies to all forms of offenses against us—including sexual transgressions committed with others.

While it is generally my advice to keep past offenses in the past (except in confessing to priesthood leaders), the whole advent of AIDS has, in some cases, changed things. Now it can literally be a life-and-death matter whether your intended husband or wife has abstained from sexual contact outside of marriage. If there is any possibility that either partner has been exposed to the HIV virus, proper medical testing should be obtained, and concerns should be discussed openly and forthrightly long before the marriage is scheduled.

Of course, it is not legally required to reveal past sins to a prospective spouse. But in many states, it is required that you disclose (1) a previous marriage, (2) bearing or fathering a child out of wedlock, (3) a past criminal record or imprisonment, and (4) having a communicable disease or (5) having been addicted to drugs and not giving evidence of a cure. All of these, in some states, are justification for annulment if they are discovered after the marriage has been performed.

7. If you have committed sexual sin in the past, how long must you wait before going to the temple?

Some young Latter-day Saints have naively believed that they could simply sin, quickly repent, and then, soon after, go on missions or get married in the temple. This, of course, is a misunderstanding. Church leaders are not trying to keep Latter-day Saints who have sinned out of the temple. They just want to make sure they are repentant and ready to make serious temple covenants with the Lord—including a covenant of chastity. Usually the period of waiting is several months and can last a year or even longer depending on the circumstances.

There are several factors that contribute to the length of time that must pass before a transgressor may go on a mission or enter or return to the temple: (1) The degree of sincere repentance, (2) whether or not a male holds the Melchizedek Priesthood, (3) whether or not the erring person has previously been through the temple, (4) whether or not similar sins have occurred in the past, and how often, and (5) whether or not the offending party is a Church officer or leader.

8. If I have had sex while still single, will it affect my future marriage?

Without question, there are serious consequences of sex outside of marriage, as noted in Chapter Six. The degree to which sex before marriage can or will affect a marriage depends on (1) how many times it occurred, (2) how many sexual partners there were, and (3) with whom it occurred, meaning, did it happen with the person he/she eventually married? If a young couple had a sexual relationship with each other just once prior to their marriage, it would have far less effect on their marriage than if one or both had sexual relationships several times with several partners prior to marriage. In such cases, it is often very difficult for the transgressors to remain true in marriage—unfortunately, habituation often continues well into the marriage. This is another good argument for sexual abstinence before marriage: so a couple can learn about intimate matters in marriage *only* with each other.

9. Are victims of rape, incest, or child sexual molestation guilty of sin? Have they "lost their virtue"?

According to my understanding, victims of sexual assault or sexual abuse are not, in that thing, guilty of sin. Instead, they are victims both of criminal acts and of sins, rather than participants in them. Elder Rex D. Pinegar of the First Quorum of the Seventy wrote an important article on this topic entitled "Let God Judge between Me and Thee." (See *Ensign,* Oct. 1981, pp. 32–35.) In the article he quoted Deuteronomy 22:25–26, noting that men who commit rape should be held accountable according to the laws of the land. But the same scripture notes "but unto the damsel thou shalt do nothing. There is in the damsel no sin." (P. 34.)

Elder Pinegar also notes: "[We must] realize that the innocent victim of a crime is still acceptable before the Lord, that she may still have faith in him, that his concern for her has not lessened, and that her standing in the Church has not diminished." (P. 35.)

On a similar note, a LDS clinical psychologist at BYU, Maxine Murdock, has observed: "Virtue is something that cannot be taken away from anyone; it can only be given up voluntarily. If, for example, a person is robbed, does that make him or her a thief? Or if someone takes your life, are you therefore guilty of murder? Certainly not. And of course the same is true of rape: the guilt lies with the perpetrator, not with the victim." ("When It Happens to One Among Us . . . ," *Ensign*, Oct. 1981, p. 39. See entire article, pp. 36–41.)

10. What do you do if you are afraid of having sex?

Those Latter-day Saints who lived the law of chastity before marriage will experience some natural anxiety and nervousness prior to the marriage. But if the anxieties are severe and one does not look forward to the experience, then perhaps professional counseling should be sought several months before the marriage. This would be true particularly for anyone who may have been a victim of incest, sexually molested as a child, or raped.

11. What do you do if you do not want to have sex on your honeymoon?

A wedding day is one of the happiest, yet most hectic, days people will experience in life. Some couples are so exhausted at the end of the day that neither one is ready for intimacy shortly after arriving at the motel or hotel. Sometimes relaxing, talking, cuddling, or even a short sleep will do wonders for the initiation of the sexual experience. If sexual relationships are not desired by one partner later that night (or morning) or on the honeymoon at all, but are anticipated by the other person, serious problems could result. This is definitely one area of the relationship that needs thorough discussion before the marriage and honeymoon.

We should also remember that the first two qualities of love mentioned in the scriptures are patience and kindness. (1 Cor. 15:5; Moro. 7:45.) Certainly these two attributes should be present during this sensitive time of the honeymoon.

12. What is the best way to avoid embarrassment on the honeymoon?

I have always been impressed with the statement in Genesis 2:25 that Adam and Eve were naked and "not ashamed." Being patient and kind on a honeymoon, not proceeding too quickly, and having a little sense of humor can do much to alleviate embarrassment.

In addition, there are many informative books a couple can read just a few weeks before the marriage that will give some insight into what awaits them. Such books include *The Act of Marriage: The Beauty of Sexual Love* (Grand Rapids, Michigan: Zondervan, 1976), by Tim and Beverly LaHaye, who are Christian writers; *Sensible Sex* (Salt Lake City: Publishers Press, 1968), by Lindsay Curtis, an LDS physician; and *Just for Newlyweds* (Salt Lake City: Deseret Book, 1992), by the author. (And may I also add that having the room pitch black, with all the lights out, will do a great deal to alleviate some of the initial embarrassment or anxiety. . . .)

13. What is the relationship between sex in marriage and spirituality?

A few Latter-day Saints have been reared with or taught the philosophy that "sex is evil/dirty" and have a difficult time with the relationship after marriage. This may also be true in regard to sex on Sunday, which is supposed to be a day of rest, relaxation, and spiritual refinement. Some biblical readers find sexuality at odds with spirituality (see Gal. 5) and cannot reconcile the two in their minds. Many Latter-day Saints, on the other hand, feel Sunday is an ideal time for sexual relationships, since rest and relaxation are essential for harmonious sexual relationships in marriage.

In a large group of several hundred Latter-day Saints, one young wife asked about the appropriateness of sexual relationships on fast Sunday, stating that when we fast we are supposed to concentrate on spiritual things rather than physical gratification. She quoted 1 Corinthians 7:2–5 as the basis for her question. President Joseph F. Smith suggested that "the law [of the fast] to the Latter-day Saints, as understood by the authorities of the Church, is that food and drink are not to be partaken of for twenty-four hours, 'from even to even,' and that the Saints are to refrain *from all bodily gratification and indulgences.*" (*Gospel Doctrine,* pp. 305–6; italics added.) Some have interpreted President Smith's remarks to include sexual relationships.

14. Is it best to leave your temple garments on during sex in marriage?

In a letter dated October 10, 1988, the First Presidency said: "Church members who have been clothed with the garment in the temple have made a covenant to wear it throughout their lives. This has been interpreted to mean that it is worn as underclothing both day and night. This sacred covenant is between the member and the Lord. Members should seek the guidance of the Holy Spirit to answer for themselves any personal questions about the wearing of the garment."

15. What is appropriate and inappropriate sexual behavior for Latter-day Saints after marriage? (Most often asked question)

Many young Latter-day Saints become aware long before they are married that there are many ways to bring about sexual stimulation, some of which may not be appropriate in an LDS marriage. The most basic general guideline is that there should be no force, coercion, or manipulation to entice a partner to participate in any sexual act. Sexual acts should be freely and spontaneously expressed in a marital relationship. Any sexual act should therefore be of mutual consent between the participating parties.

I do need to add, however, that two adults could mutually consent to a sexual act that may be (1) illegal, or (2) spiritually demeaning. Such acts should be avoided.

There are several ways a husband and wife can help enhance the sexual satisfaction in a marriage, but this requires adequate communication and a willingness to discuss intimate things.

16. How serious is oral sex before marriage?

Some young single LDS people have mistakenly believed that "oral is moral" and, along with other sexual acts, is not wrong as long as sexual intercourse does not occur. Such a belief might be called "technical virginity." The Church teaches that oral sex by single adults is a serious sexual sin, and individuals engaging in such practices will be dealt with accordingly by Church leaders.

17. What is the LDS Church's position on birth control?

Following is the statement on birth control from the LDS *General Handbook of Instructions:*

"Husbands must be considerate of their wives, who have a great responsibility not only for bearing children but also for caring for them through childhood. Husbands should help their wives conserve their health and strength. Married couples should seek inspiration from the Lord in meeting their marital challenges and rearing their children according to the teachings of the gospel." (Salt Lake City: The Church of Jesus Christ of Latter-day Saints, 1989, p. 11-4.)

Also, an article by Dr. Homer Ellsworth, an LDS physician and gynecologist, has been both helpful and informative to many Latter-day Saints. Dr. Ellsworth carefully notes the importance for LDS couples to have children. But he also observes that

if for certain personal reasons a couple prayerfully decides that having another child immediately is unwise, the method of spacing children—discounting possible medical or physical effects—makes little difference. Abstinence (rhythm method), of course, is also a form of contraception, and like any other method it has side effects, some of which are harmful to the marriage relationship. ("I Have a Question," *Ensign*, Aug. 1979, pp. 23–26.)

18. When is the best time for sex? AM? or PM?

Most couples have their own unique preferences or patterns. The "best time" for sexual relationships in a marriage is when the couple is ready and anticipating it.

19. Are there such things as sexual peaks? Such as time of day, week, year, aging?

DAILY AND MONTHLY PEAKS: There is some evidence that men peak sexually about every forty-eight hours. It has also been established that many women have sexual peaks about the time of ovulation (usually 13–15 days *before* the onset of menstruation), when estrogen is at its highest level in the hormonal system.

LIFETIME PEAKS: Males are generally in their sexual prime during their late teens and early twenties. Most females reach sexual maturity in the late twenties or early thirties.

In females, estrogen—and often sexual energy—decreases after a hysterectomy, where one or both ovaries are removed, and just before and after menopause. In these cases, female sexual energy can be restored through estrogen replacement therapy or hormonal replacement therapy.

There is some evidence that many males experience "viropause," where the level of testosterone decreases. During this time, which occurs for most men in the mid-fifties and early sixties, an erection takes more time to obtain and is more difficult to maintain. Though this is sometimes called the period of "sexual slowdown," most men continue to be sexually active, though with less frequency.

20. Do elderly people have sex?

The answer for the vast majority of "aging" couples is yes, they still do have sexual relationships, although the frequency may decline somewhat due to the aging process.

Some married couples, through mutual consent, decide not to have sexual intercourse due to accidents, illnesses, or injuries that make the act difficult and painful, if not impossible. Such couples then make other efforts to be intimate with each other; these include, but are not limited to, physical passion.

Chapter 10

MAINTAINING VISION
AND CONTROL

I would like to conclude with two stories that I hope will reinforce the things we've talked about in this book.

No Control, No Vision

When I was a ten-year-old boy growing up in Centerfield, Utah, I had an experience that gave me some noticeable scars on my left arm—scars that are still there. It's quite a story about how I got those scars.

When I was growing up, my father, Alvin Barlow, ran a small grocery story and gas station in Centerfield. It was called Barlow Service. Dad later claimed he was years ahead of the "gas and groceries" concept that caught on later with several national chain stores. As a young boy I spent a great deal of time in the grocery store working with my father, my grandfather Altheron Barlow, my Aunt Erma (Brough), and my Uncle Lloyd (Schow), all of whom worked at the store at different times.

One of my jobs as a ten year old was to walk two blocks over to the Centerfield Post Office where Dean Malmgren, the postmaster, would put the mail for the store in a large paper sack I took with me. I would then return and give the mail to my father. After several weeks of going for the mail I got bored with walking and asked my older sister, Jane, age fourteen, if I could borrow her new blue bicycle and ride it the two blocks to pick up the mail. She had reservations at first (typical of sisters). After all, the bicycle was *hers,* and it was brand new. After constant begging and, as I recall, some kind of bargaining, I finally got Jane to agree. Before she let me take it, she gave me a strict lecture on being careful not to mar or scratch her new bicycle. I nonchalantly agreed and took off.

After a few weeks of riding Jane's bike for the mail, I got bored again. So I decided to get even more daring and create a little more excitement and thrill for myself. I practiced riding the new blue bike without my hands on the handlebars. I got pretty good at it, too. After a few weeks of practice I could ride the entire two blocks without holding onto the handlebars. (I should add that I had to pass through an intersection!) So back and forth I went, day after day, riding Jane's bike to pick up the mail with no hands on the handlebars.

But guess what? After a while that also got tedious and boring for a ten-year-old country boy, so I decided I needed more of a challenge. What would add a little more intrigue and zest to my life? I finally decided I would practice riding the bicycle with no hands on the handlebars—and my eyes shut!

Very few people had done that (now I know why!), but few also know a young boy's thrill of riding down a country sidewalk on a bicycle with little control and no vision. It was a sensational experience! I got so good at it that I could ride the entire two blocks, pass through the intersection (I would listen for cars, pickups, or tractors), pick up the mail from Brother Malmgren, and then ride back to the store—all with eyes closed and no hands on the handlebars. I did this for several days, unbeknown to either my sister or my dad.

If you ever happen to drive through Centerfield, Utah, today, traveling on highway 89, you'll notice a sheep pasture on the east side of the road, about midway through town. You'll also see a barbed-wire fence around it. That pasture and that fence were also there when I was a boy, owned at the time by Chris Sorenson. At one time, that barbed wire fence was indented. I put that dent there—with my sister's new blue bicycle.

One morning my dad asked me, again, to go for the mail. I got on Jane's bike and took off, with no hands on the handlebars and eyes shut. I was getting good at this. I rode through the intersection, got the mail, and started back on the sidewalk—little control and no vision. What a momentary thrill! But this time, as I passed Chris Sorenson's sheep pasture, the front bike tire hit a stone on the sidewalk. I felt the sensation of the bike tipping over, but it was too late. I could not get control of the bicycle in time. I landed on the barbed wire with my left arm and cannot describe the painful sensation. The new bike followed and got all scratched up.

I left Jane's bike all tangled up in the fence, picked up the paper sack filled with mail, and ran crying to my dad. I will never forget the moment I found him. I held up my bleeding arm to him, tears streaming from my eyes, expecting some words of comfort. (Not only was he my dad, but he was my bishop at the time.)

"What happened, son?" he asked, as he examined my arm.

"I was riding Jane's bike on the sidewalk without holding onto the handlebars," I confided. "And," I added, "I had my eyes shut."

Dad paused for a moment and then said something I needed to hear. With all the wisdom and insight of a concerned father and bishop, he muttered, "YOU BIG DUMBBELL!" He then suggested I go home and ask mom to patch up my arm, which I did.

Does this story have application to our discussion on sexual abstinence before marriage? I think so. And I hope each reader will remember it. When it comes to sexual behavior, I believe many young Latter-day Saints today are riding down the pathway of life with little or no control—and with their eyes shut. Few are aware of the potential harm and pain that such actions can bring to their lives. But such harm and pain will surely come. All it takes is some brief moment when a small rock on the sidewalk throws them into circumstances they had not anticipated and cannot control.

Like myself on the bicycle, they may have some momentary pleasure and sensation, with little or no vision of what could eventually happen. But remember the biblical admonition that "where there is no vision, the people perish." (Prov. 29:18.) To such young people may I suggest you open your eyes and take note of where you are—and, if necessary, get control of the situation! The Lord has indicated we will never be tempted beyond our ability to resist, because he will help us. But we must take advantage of his help. (See 1 Cor. 10:13.) However wicked and perverse the world becomes, young Latter-day Saints can face the future with confidence: The Lord always stands ready to help us. The Lord has commanded and warned that we should wait until marriage to experience sexual relations. Like Nephi of old, we too should be willing to "go and do the things which the Lord hath commanded, for . . . the Lord giveth no commandments unto the children of men, save he shall prepare a way for them that they may accomplish the thing which he commandeth them." (1 Ne. 3:7.)

And to those who give no thought to sexual abstinence before marriage, to those who desire the temporary sensations of pleasure with little or no regard to the potential pain, I simply reiterate what my father said to me when I injured my arm.

Amnon and Tamar

The second story I would like to tell happened to someone else. It is a biblical account that occurred thousands of years ago, yet it is contemporary and modern in application. Apparently many young people in all ages (and old people, for that matter) can confuse lust and love. When our hormones are operating at full force we may feel attracted to someone and initially think it is love. And it could indeed be love. Or it could be just plain lust.

In my Preparation for Marriage classes at BYU we talk about the Blocked-Sex Theory of Love Development. I explain it like this: When we are physically or sexually attracted to someone and the feelings are "blocked" or not acted upon, tensions arise, and these tensions are often identified as love. The blocking or lack of action comes from a variety of sources, including religious restraints, family and personal values, unpleasant sexual experiences from the past, or the unwillingness of a partner to cooperate.

If the sexual attraction is great, and the blocking is in operation, the tensions will usually be high. At that point we may think we "really are in love." By the same reasoning, when the attraction is great, and the "blocks" are ignored (e.g., sexual relationships are experienced), the tension is thereby reduced and what one or both once thought was love vanishes away. During my nearly twenty-five years of working with more than fifteen thousand young people, many of whom were Latter-day Saints, I have seen this phenomenon occur again and again. A couple was physically attracted to each other, the "blocks" were there (religious, family, or personal), and the sexual tension was mistakenly identified as love when, in reality, it was mostly lust. At some point, the sexual experience occurred, the tension was reduced, and what was identified as love then disappeared. Sometimes it disappeared immediately.

Nowhere is this occurrence more dramatically illustrated than in the Old Testament story of Amnon and Tamar. (She is identified as his "sister," but it appears she was a half-sister. See 2 Sam. 13:1–17.) The account states that Amnon loved Tamar so much that he was sick, but he was also "vexed" because she was a virgin and he didn't want to do anything sexually with her. (Vv. 1–2.)

But now comes the peer influence. Amnon had a friend named Jonadab who the scripture states "was a very subtil man." (V. 3.) Jonadab asked Amnon why he was sick and losing so much weight, to which Amnon simply replied, "I love Tamar. . . ." (V. 4.) Sensing Amnon's sexual frustration, Jonadab, in essence, suggested he need not wait and encouraged Amnon to go into his bedroom and pretend he was sick. Then he should ask if Tamar could bring food to the bedroom, where Amnon could enact his sexual desires. (V. 5.)

So Amnon followed the suggestion of his "subtle" friend, "made himself sick," and requested that Tamar come to his bedroom with food. Tamar, unaware of his intentions, prepared some food for Amnon and took it to his home. After she arrived, Amnon sent everyone in the household away so they could be alone. (Vv. 6–9.) Amnon then asked her to come into his bedroom to help him eat (an insight to stay out of bedrooms). Tamar unwisely obliged and went into his bedroom, where he took hold of her and gave the age-old invitation, "Come lie with me." (Vv. 10–11.)

Tamar resisted his advances, saying, "Nay, my brother, do not force me; for no such thing ought to be done in Israel; do not thou this folly. And I, whither shall I cause my shame to go? And as for thee, thou shalt be as one of the fools in Israel."

(Vv. 12–13.) She argued that they should marry first—then they could lawfully engage in sexual relations.

Now follow the precipitous act and consequences (remember the Blocked-Sex Theory of Love Development):

"Howbeit he would not hearken unto her voice; but, being stronger than she, forced her, and lay with her." (V. 14.)

And what was the immediate consequence? Did Amnon really love Tamar? Or did he confuse love with lust, as so many have done before and since? Read the tragic conclusion to the episode:

"Then [immediately] Amnon hated her exceedingly; so that the hatred with which he hated her was greater than the love wherewith he had loved her. And Amnon said unto her, Arise, [get out of bed,] be gone." (V. 15.) Now notice what Amnon does next. Not only has he committed a sexual sin, but he then abandons Tamar as well. She pleads, "There is no cause; this evil in sending me away is greater than the other that thou didst unto me. But he would not hearken unto her. Then he called his servant that ministered unto him, and said, Put now this woman out from me, and bolt the door after her." (Vv. 16–17.)

"Bridle All Your Passions"

I can't think of a better story with which to conclude, as I repeat my plea for sexual abstinence before marriage. Let's return one more time to the scripture quoted at the beginning of this book: "See that ye bridle all your passions, that ye may be filled with love." (Alma 38:12.) When sexual passions are not bridled, they can overpower or distort a relationship as happened with Amnon and Tamar. By "bridling our passions" before marriage, we can focus our attention on other important aspects of the relationship that will be crucial to a successful, stable, satisfying marriage. People can be "in lust" rather than "in love" and fool themselves into believing that the resulting tension is love. In fact, people can be physically attracted to individuals they not only don't love, but don't like! That is why Alma's admonition to "bridle our passions" is still relevant. When the sexual aspect of a relationship is not controlled, we have little opportunity to learn about ("be filled with") other important aspects of love.

If the reader chooses just one part of this book to remember or review when contemplating the reasons for sexual abstinence before marriage, I hope it will be this account of Amnon and Tamar. It is an ancient story with a modern application. Hopefully, we too can "liken the scriptures unto ourselves for our own profit and learning." (1 Ne. 19:23.) As I previously noted, we *can* learn from OPE (Other People's Experiences). Maybe young Latter-day Saints can also understand early in life why "wickedness never was happiness," as the errant Corianton learned "by sad experience." (See Alma 41:10; D&C 121:39.)

Will parents, youth, and youth leaders be able to meet the challenges in the future? Will each generation help the next be ready for what lies ahead in the last days as we prepare for the second coming of the Lord Jesus Christ?

In 1990 the First Presidency of the Church gave us this needful challenge: "We pray that you—the young and rising generation—will keep your bodies and minds clean, free from the contaminations of the world, that you will be fit and pure vessels to bear triumphantly the responsibilities of the kingdom of God *in preparation for the second coming of our Savior.*" (*For the Strength of Youth,* pp. 4–5; italics added. Used by permission.)

May all Latter-day Saints, young and old alike, strive to become the "pure people" the Lord is trying to raise up in righteousness before him in the last days. (D&C 110:16.)

For if not us, who? And if not now, when?

Index

Abstinence, premarital sexual: importance of, 7–8; reasons for, 34, 41–42, 79, 127; increases freedom, 80; during engagement, 100–107; and second virginity, 116–17
Abuse: sexual, 19; victims, 129–30
Acquired Immune Deficiency Syndrome (AIDS), 11, 35–37, 41–42, 80, 128
Addiction, sexual, 51–52
Adultery, 8, 51, 83–84, 125–26
Advertisements, 29–30
Affection, genuine, 124
Agency, 93
Aggression, 26
Alma the elder, 109–10
Alma the younger, 109, 112
Amnon, 141–42
Analogies, teaching, 65–66, 114–15
Anxiety, sexual, 130
Atonement, 68–70, 115
Attraction, sexual, 50–51, 124–25

Augustine, 45

Bedrooms, 102–3, 107
Bicycle, story of, 136–39
Birth control, 133–34
Birth, premature, 38
Bishop, meeting with, 105–6. *See also* Confession, Priesthood leaders
Blocks, sexual, 140–42
Book of Mormon, 16
Bubble gum analogy, 65

Cake analogy, 65
Car dashboard analogy, 86
Chastity, law of, 13, 92, 108, 117
Children, 61–62, 126, 134
Chlamydia, 35, 37–38
Christian, early, beliefs, 45
Church of Jesus Christ of Latter-Day Saints, The: position on sexual purity, 7–8; concern over media, 30–32; position on self-stimulation, 48–49, 53–55, 57; position on